Miracles
do Happen:

To Clark and
Kathy
Lovely memories of your
visit to our parish
Fr. Ernie Smith
7. 8. 94

Miracles
do Happen:
a priest called Smith

Ernie Smith

Foreword by **Ed Campion**

CollinsDove
A Division of HarperCollins*Publishers*

Published by Collins Dove
A Division of HarperCollins*Publishers* (Australia) Pty Ltd
22–24 Joseph Street
North Blackburn, Victoria 3130

First published 1993
Designed by William Hung
Cover design by William Hung
Cover photograph Carolyn Johns

Typeset by Collins Dove Publishers
Printed in Australia by Griffin Paperbacks Pty Ltd

The National Library of Australia
Cataloguing-in-Publication Data:

Smith, Ernie, 1939–
Miracles do happen.

ISBN 1 86371 233 X.

1. Smith, Ernie, 1939–   . 2. Sacred Heart Mission (St. Kilda, Vic.) —
Biography. 3. Catholic Church — Victoria — Clergy — Biography.
4. Priests — Victoria — Biography. 5. Missionaries — Victoria —
Biography. I. Title.

282.092

CONTENTS

FOREWORD

People who think the Church is dying ought to read this book.
It brims with life. It is about ways the Church can open people
to a richer life by uncovering their hidden unused gifts. The
author, Ernie Smith, employs the word 'gift' again and again,
often in unexpected ways. People's gifts might appear when
they are broken or hurt or difficult. Often the most destitute
are coaxed into life by the love and care of the local parish.

And what a model of a parish, not the arid religious service
station of ill repute lorded over by a bossy insensitive cleric.
The parish and the Mission form an 'open house' community
of active Christians who enjoy using their diverse talents as a
team serving Christ in the world. Two things mark the people
of this book. The first is their respect for the 'specialness' of
those they serve; everyone is unique. The second thing you
notice about these people is their joy. They enjoy what they
are doing. This is a sure sign that God is with them.

It is noticeable too how well the bishops appear in this
book. Bishop-bashing is an old and customary sport for those
who write about the church. Not here. The bishops featured in
this account exhibit the rare talent of listening to what people

are saying. Then they offer counsel and the precious gift of encouragement. One bishop is even heard telling why he is happy being a bishop. All of this strikes a new note in Australian writing.

This book is most remarkable for the picture it gives of Ernie Smith himself—a man grateful for the parents and grandparents who taught him about belonging to a local community and to the Young Christian Worker movement which, more than the seminary, made him the priest he is. Here is a brave self-portrait of a man who is honest about his own emotions—how loving someone can hurt you horribly especially when they die. Tears come into the story often, for tears are part of life. Laughter too is shared and often about Ernie himself.

This book will give heart to anyone who may be starting to think that the Church has lost its way. It takes you, not to textbooks about the Church or to theological theories, but to the real life of modern Australian Catholicism. It shows that there is plenty of life and hence plenty of hope in at least one parish. We are all in debt to Ernie Smith for lighting a torch which can show us the way into the future.

Edmund Campion

INTRODUCTION

It's important for me as a writer and also for you as a reader to know why this book is being written. There are so many reasons for not writing. After all, who am I to write a book? Is my story really all that important? Do I consider myself an expert? Who am I writing for? And why?

I first wrote the manuscript during 1981 as a narration of the various ways in which we had experimented with parish ministry in Yarraville. In the meantime there has been a development in the ministry of the Church here in West St Kilda where I have been since 1982. This 1993 version brings up-to-date the ways in which I along with lay people working together as a team, have endeavoured to be a church ministering in the world today. I hope that the story of my experiences as a priest ministering with others, particularly in the parishes of Yarraville and West St Kilda, is one of encouragement to people involved, or wishing to be involved, in ministering in the Church today and in the future.

I do not propose that the way in which our teams have worked in Yarraville and West St Kilda is THE model for parish ministry. However, I am confident that what has been accomplished and is still being accomplished is one of many different models for the local church today and in the future.

How we minister depends to a great degree upon our personal background. The early chapters are simply a portrait of my own background. When the publisher asked me to write a bit about myself, I managed a couple of pages but was sent off to write some more. These were the most difficult chapters to write.

I will tell my story, attempting to recall as accurately as possible not only events or decisions but the feelings and reasonings at the time. If in retrospect I add more to events than was present at the time, then I will have to ask your forgiveness. Events recalled do have the habit of growing larger in one's mind, much as that big fish which you caught many years ago.

I am not writing a literary work, and in fact this was not my best subject at school. How I write is how I speak! I sometimes speak too fast, often with the use of slang or colloquialisms and also with a tendency to wander all over the place—that's me!

The pages which follow are not meant to be a theological treatise on the nature of the Church. The reflections and stories recall a journey of one priest with the people in his life. It has been with and through these people that my understanding of ministry and my compassion for those in need has widened.

I am indebted to many people just for the fact that this book was even started. People encouraged me to write this, in particular, lay people who have been my friends over a long time and who have always shown interest and given support to my ventures, even if they may have seemed pipe dreams. To the lay people, my friends, who have kept at me and supported me in the decision to write, thanks a lot.

Most of all I must say thanks to the people who have worked with me through the years in Yarraville and West St Kilda. There have been many people who have been part of the dream of Ernie Smith coming to fruition. You will meet these people as I tell the story.

In the beginning there were Thelma, Bernie, Colleen, Joan and others in Yarraville. At West St Kilda, things got underway with Kate, Cathy, Pat and a host of volunteers. Today there are more than fifty people working with me. In the years between there have been many others who have worked with me, some for a short time, some for a longer time, all have been part of building a model of parish and team work. To all of you who have worked with me, thanks for the time that our lives have been joined together—past, present and future.

To the lay people of Yarraville and West St Kilda, thanks for taking up your mission in the Church. Much of this story is really about you.

PART 1

Stories of today

CHAPTER 1

When Dreams Become Reality

The place—Bethlehem hospital, a hospice for people terminally ill with cancer. The time—Thursday evening, 25 July, 1985. Cath Stewart and I are in the room of Kevin Cockerall who is dying from a brain tumour. Cath has worked in St Kilda at Sacred Heart Mission from the beginning. Cath and I have been closest to Kevin, sharing life with him in our parish home. During the rest of the evening, while Kevin lies unconscious, the team of people with whom we work in West St Kilda parish gradually drift into the hospital. Around midnight we are all gathered together around Kevin's bedside. Kevin died peacefully, around 5.00 a.m. on Friday morning. We adjourn back to the Mission House at West St Kilda to be with each other and to share our grief, our hope and our relief that Kevin's suffering is at last over.

During this evening and the weeks before, I had been aware of the gift of working with a team of people. The story of Kevin in his sickness brings out many of the significant aspects of working as a team in parish ministry. We were a varied group of people gathered around Kevin's bedside. Each of us had come to St Kilda in response to a personal need or with some sort of challenge to be faced. On this night we were one with each other.

The story of Kevin Cockerall is so simple but so significant. Who was he? Why do I see him as so important? Kevin had arrived at the Mission quite awhile before. He was something of a loner and had come to the parish hall for the free daily meal. He began to come regularly and eventually became one of the constant helpers with the meals service. Kevin would arrive in the morning and take his position at the big sink. There he would begin the task of peeling a mountain of potatoes for the day's meal. When that was finished he began the task of cleaning up around the cooking area. He would then have an early lunch with the other helpers so that he could be ready to start the big wash up. And big it was, because at that time we were serving over 200 meals a day. The sink belonged to Kevin; this was his domain. He was an industrious little fellow and worked hard at his jobs. Such jobs would not rate among the most glamorous or sought-after chores in the hall.

Kevin's fiftieth birthday was earlier in 1985. We always try to remember the big 'O' birthdays, so on Kevin's fiftieth I arrived at the hall with a birthday cake. The shy and quiet Kevin immediately bolted into the back pantry among the vegetables. I retrieved him and carried him over my shoulder back into the dining room where we all sang happy birthday as Kevin hung over my shoulder. Full of embarrassment, but still in his own way delighted, Kevin blew out the candles, cut the cake and distributed it. Such moments recognise the important place of every person among us.

A few weeks later I received a call from a social worker at St John of God Hospital in Ballarat some seventy miles from Melbourne. She told me that Mr Cockerall would like to let me know that he was in hospital and had a brain tumour. I began by saying that I didn't know any Mr Cockerall. It was only after a description of Kevin that I realised who Mr Cockerall was.

The story then unfolded. A few days before Kevin had been at a hostel where he had collapsed and been admitted to the hospital. Kevin had been told the day before that he had an inoperable brain tumour. At first he conveyed to the social worker that there was no one for him to tell about this news. However, the next day he changed his mind. 'Perhaps Father Smith at Sacred Heart Mission would like to know' he told the social worker. And so the phone call.

We certainly wanted to know. The following morning I went with Eric Robertson to Ballarat to visit Kevin and work out what needed to be done for him in the way of care. The diagnosis was confirmed by the doctor to Kevin in our presence. Kevin spoke with us about how he felt and what he wanted to do. It was a sad time for Eric and me as we chatted with Kevin about how to best live out his life.

The following Monday, 4 March, Kevin was transferred to Melbourne to receive treatment and to undergo surgery which would bring him some comfort in his illness. We had no idea where this journey was to lead us, but we knew one thing for sure . . . Kevin was a part of our 'family'. Whatever was needed, we would be able to do it.

At this stage I was his 'next of kin'. We didn't know of any family and he was not about to tell us anything. There are many people like Kevin who, for one reason or another, have become loners and have cut themselves off from their families. We always try to respect that position.

For the next couple of weeks Kevin received treatment at two city hospitals. People from the Mission were his only visitors. After this treatment arrangements were made for Kevin to go to Bethlehem Hospital where he would receive special care. So far, so good.

Kevin wanted to come and live with us at our house in St Kilda, but we knew that this was impossible. We could not care for Kevin. We couldn't offer 24-hour assistance, or the nursing or bathing care he required. It was impossible and that question was a closed issue. At least that's what we thought! Despite Kevin's protests he had to go to Bethlehem Hospital for the care he needed.

On his first weekend leave from Bethlehem Hospital, Kevin came to stay with us. Sick and dying as he was, he absconded. In pyjamas and dressing gown, without money, complete with walking stick, he vanished. We had a terrible Sunday afternoon and evening trying to find him, wondering where he could possibly be. On Monday morning, he turned up at his bank.

When Pat Johnson went to bring Kevin home she got a burst of abuse, and he waved his walking stick at her. Eventually we brought him home, contacted the hospital who sent the nursing supervisor and we sat down for a heart-to-heart talk. Before this, I had given him a bit of a telling-off for his treatment of us all and of Pat in particular. I felt horrible scolding someone who was dying.

After a couple of hours a compromise was reached. The deal was that Kevin would stay with us until he was not well enough to be cared for at home. The nursing sisters would come each day to bathe him and give the necessary medication. Only after the sisters had gone did I realise that 'compromise' meant that we were doing exactly what Kevin had wanted in the first place, and that which we knew we couldn't do.

For the next few weeks Kevin stayed with us in our home. On most days he visited the hall to see his friends. He enjoyed being with us, and we certainly enjoyed having him. We entered into a whole new level of relationship and care with

Kevin, not only those of us living with him, but the entire Mission team.

Eventually, as his condition worsened, we knew and he knew that the time had come to go to Bethlehem Hospital. He agreed, but again came his conditions. We agreed to pick him up each day at 9.30 a.m. and take him back at 5.00 p.m. Again we were about to do what seemed impossible, but by now it wasn't an issue because we had grown so close together.

Each day for the next few weeks someone from the team would be at the hospital at 9.30 a.m., and someone would return him to the hospital at 5.00 p.m. The sisters would come with the necessary injection around midday. The parlour of the Mission House was turned into a bedroom. If Kevin were well enough, he would be sitting up receiving visitors; if he was not well he could stay in bed and sleep or whatever. All of a sudden the open house was centering around Kevin.

As time progressed, Kevin became weaker. At the suggestion of the sisters at the hospital, it was left to Cathy or me to pick up Kevin and take him home. He was by now close to death, but he was still determined to come out each day. The sisters at the hospital were quite happy for this arrangement to continue and gave us some special advice. Kevin may die in the car. If this happens on the way to the Mission, then simply turn around and come back. If it happens on the way back, then just keep on coming to the hospital!!

There were some interesting times during this period. A social worker at the hospice had upset Kevin by insisting that he had to make a will. For some reason this really got to Kevin. He was hopping mad about it. After a chat, I convinced him that the only reason to make a will was to get rid of his possessions. If we spent his money, there would be no need for a will. He thought that this was a good idea, and we swung into action. In fact, the only money he had was what he had saved while in the hospital. He made a 'shopping list' which included a gift for his friend Hazel, something for Cathy and two cassette recorders for the hospice. I had suggested a small colour television, but Kevin felt that two recorders would be better because when you are sick, you can listen to music.

I bought the recorders, and on a Sunday morning we headed off to the art and craft market on the St Kilda Esplanade. We bought gifts, cards and some cakes for morning tea and gift-giving back at our house. We returned to the hospital where Kevin gave the recorders to the sisters. These were precious moments at the time and equally precious memories to recall. What I didn't know was that Kevin had planned with Cathy to get me a gift as well. That surprise gave Kevin a great thrill.

Kevin's great determination came to a head on the Wednesday before he died. When I arrived to bring him to the Mission, I was told by the sister that he would not be able to go out because he had almost died an hour before. He was now close to death. But when I saw Kevin, he insisted that he was coming out again. He threatened that if I didn't take him, he would walk out. This was his usual threat. After a glance at the sister and having received an appropriate nod, I said 'okay', picked him up in my arms and carried him to the car.

Kevin came to the Mission, but by midday he was so ill that he had to return to the hospital. Many of the people associated with our Mission came to say their goodbye to Kevin. Everyone knew, including Kevin, that this was his last goodbye to the Mission. Cathy and I returned with him to the hospital and stayed with him until he died on the following Friday morning.

This was a precious time for all of us who had come to know, love and care for Kevin. It was a climactic point in my dreams—a team of people working together in ministry. Together, we had come to know and love Kevin. Together we had cared for him. Along the way we had involved many people in the care of Kevin.

The very beginning of our relationship with Kevin had come through the hospitality extended by the Mission—first through the daily meal provided in our hall and then through the welcome of the 'Open House' where people were able to come to our house for a cuppa. It was this hospitality and welcome which had enabled Kevin to become involved in the life of the Mission and to find a purpose in his lonely life. He had shown us that we can do far more than we imagine is possible with the help of people around us. By living with other people in a house down the street, I had been given the privilege of taking Kevin into our home.

So many facets of team were involved in our journey with Kevin over those few months of sickness. He taught us and came close to us. There have been many other 'Kevins' in our life and work together here at Sacred Heart Mission in West St Kilda, but the story of Kevin is important to me as it brings many of those points into a clear focus.

CHAPTER 2

'Bread and Blessing'

In July 1988 a one-hour documentary entitled 'Bread and Blessing' was shown on television and depicted some areas of ministry undertaken by Sacred Heart Mission at West St Kilda. Put together by the Catholic Communications Office, it presented, in a sensitive manner, a ministry by the Church which could easily have been sensationalised.

I had been invited to be part of such a documentary earlier but had always declined because of the sensitive areas of our work in St Kilda. The team of people working with me at this time struggled with the question of sensitivity and privacy, but we eventually agreed to be part of such a documentary with the provision that nothing would be shown without our approval. I was impressed by the completed documentary. I felt proud of all the people involved in the Mission. There was much shown and presented in a good light.

Sacred Heart Mission today

There are times when the growth of the Mission to its present size comes crashing in on me. This can be somewhat frightening. Just recently the Mission was struggling to find the way to overcome an operating deficit of $160,000. This is a far cry from the simple beginnings of the Mission in St Kilda. In early 1993 there was a Mission team of over fifty people which included both religious and lay people, some full-time and others part-time, with a total yearly wages bill of over $800,000.

During 1992 word was received from the Federal Health Department that we had been approved for a Government grant to purchase a hostel. We were to receive $1.15 million as a capital grant. The property, once purchased, would belong to our Mission. This was wonderful news, but also a reminder of how the Mission had grown both in size and credibility over the years.

New forms and models of management needed to be introduced as our growth increased over the past few years. It was no longer possible for a small team of people to meet together and have overall responsibility for the Mission. The ministries in the Mission had expanded, the team had grown in size, the administration was an increasing question, communication was more difficult. These are real issues to be faced.

Before sharing the story of the Mission over the years, perhaps it is appropriate to begin with a good description of Sacred Heart Mission as it is today.

Open House The 'Open House' approach was the starting point to the work of the Mission and is still a focus today. I arrived with Kate Wilson in 1982. Kate was a young woman who had first crossed my path when I was a chaplain to the Young Christian Student's Movement (YCS) in the early 1970s. Kate was a young student from one of the Melbourne parishes. After completing her secondary schooling, I invited Kate to work full-time for this student movement. Following this, Kate began a social welfare course at the university and lived in our Community House in Yarraville. As providence would have it, she completed her degree just as I moved to St Kilda. I offered her a rather undefined job which she accepted. We quite literally opened the front door together and people came in.

Things have changed somewhat, but basically the same approach of welcome and hospitality is extended to anyone who comes to the Mission House (the former presbytery). There has been an 'Open House' ministry on certain mornings and evenings each week. People are free to drop in for a cuppa and a chat, to enjoy the hospitality of the Mission and the company of other people (including volunteers), to simply stop for awhile or to seek advice or help. In 1992 this ministry transferred to a much larger activity centre in our hall which gives greater opportunity to care for people. It is conducted almost entirely by volunteers who come at various rostered times.

The areas of involvement by the Mission have broadened, but the spirit of hospitality developed in the early days remains.

The daily meal From the 'Open House' approach we moved into sharing lunch with people in our kitchen. Over the years this has also grown. Today there is a daily meal catering for an average of over 300 people each day. In 1983 the meal service moved to the parish hall. Today it is conducted by full-time workers and plenty of volunteers. The volunteers come from the people themselves who arrive for a meal and from parishioners of St Kilda and other parishes.

As the numbers coming to lunch continued to grow in those early days, we found ourselves with something of a dilemma. With fifty or more people coming for lunch, things were a trifle crowded—the table seated only twelve!! For three or four months we struggled with the question of a suitable location. The intimacy of eating around the kitchen table was as important as the food we were sharing. But eventually we were forced to move to the supper room of the big parish hall. There we could adequately seat seventy people at one time.

We learned something from this important move. We were placing too much emphasis on our own contribution in care. When we moved, we discovered how much the people could care for each other. We never regretted this relocation after all the worry about the shift.

The cooks at this time were people from the parish and the parish team. We all pitched in and gave a hand to prepare the daily meal. During this time, I frequented the Footscray market where I bought trays of meat at very reduced prices at the end of the market day. The butcher came to know me as the guy buying all the trays of sausages, mince and chops. Eventually I was able to work out a deal with him to buy the leftovers every Saturday.

Sick or elderly people
St Kilda has many sick and elderly people, many of whom are living alone. From the beginning, a great effort has gone into the care of these people, to make them feel part of our community and to make sure that they are not left alone.

This care began, as in my previous parishes, with a special Mass for our sick or elderly people and was held at the convent. This has continued to be a source of strength and care for our old and sick people. We have met in various venues during the past eleven years. At present we meet in our small subsidiary church of Our Lady of Dolours each fortnight. Between seventy and eighty people attend this Mass to which they are brought by volunteer drivers, some of whom have been regularly involved since the first of these Masses.

Communion to sick people at home is that form of care which has been entrusted to ministers of the Eucharist. These ministers bring Communion to people in their own home or in the many houses of special accommodation. These houses have been a particular challenge to us. The people living there are among the poorest of our community, having poor health, no money, no home and often no family. The aim of the Sacred Heart Mission has been to tap into this loneliness, isolation and lack of resources and do whatever we can to give these people's lives more meaning.

Our involvement with and care for lonely, sick people has continued to develop. There is an increasing variety of activities for them through art, recreation, music and outings.

Art in the community In 1987 we employed Sister Rose Derrick, a Presentation Sister, to conduct sessions of art for the people in the houses of special accommodation. Held on a weekly basis, these classes proved to be invaluable in stimulating people who otherwise would just be sitting around and doing nothing. As Sister Rose herself stated in the documentary 'Bread and Blessing', 'Many live impoverished lives and the art session has been one way of breaking into this loneliness and isolation'.

The walls of the Mission House and the hall meals centre are now adorned with various art treasures which have come from the Monday morning art classes conducted by Sister Rose in our community centre. The paintings themselves are an education because although many of them could be said to be childlike, many also show an incredible depth of knowledge of art and perspective. Some of the beautiful landscapes have been painted by people who are severely afflicted, either physically or mentally. These paintings give a glimpse of what may have been or could have been for these people.

Providing people with the opportunity to express themselves through art is a simple ministry with extraordinary results.

Crisis support An area of care in all parishes is to provide material aid. In St Kilda this need is a high priority. The question of how best to provide material aid in the form of food, clothing, vouchers, furniture or financial assistance, has been a constant challenge from the first days of the Mission. We have endeavoured not to be simply a 'hand-out' agency, but to see the call for material assistance as an invitation to respond immediately with care and look beyond to other areas of need in a person's life.

As the need has grown, the Mission has developed in its response. One of our parish houses is now the centre for all material assistance. One of our team is the coordinator and another group of volunteers has been drawn together to take responsibility for this ministry.

Opportunity shop To help in the area of material aid, an opportunity shop was established in the parish. It serves primarily as a huge wardrobe so that we always have clothing, blankets and cooking utensils on hand for people in need. Over the years we have operated shops at three different places, but now the parish hall has become a giant opportunity shop. As well as providing us with this wardrobe, the shop has also become an invaluable source of revenue for the many other needs the Mission meets.

The wonderful level of support of people and from people providing goods has been a great asset for the Mission. It means that we can respond immediately. Again, the volunteers have made this ministry work. A second group of volunteers from one of the parishes of Melbourne has since offered to manage an Op Shop for us in another suburb.

Outreach St Kilda is well known as a place of prostitution, drug addiction and homelessness. Over the years our efforts have brought us into contact with many men and women who have been affected in these ways. Our involvement and care in these areas has grown. Counselling of individuals is part of the day-to-day operation of our Mission. Some individuals within our community have been receiving support for a long time. Caring for people that have problems with alcoholism requires a lot of patience, a sense of humour, the ability to withstand frustration and, above all, faith and hope in the person.

Some of the chronic alcoholic men around St Kilda would drive anyone to frustration. I can remember on one occasion wishing that a particular fellow would hit me so that I would have the legitimate excuse to hit him back! Thankfully he did not hit me, and the 'pleasure' was denied me. But he was so frustrating and annoying. Others, no matter what they do, can never get into your 'bad books'. They seem to have a special charm that keeps on getting at you.

Ministry to women A 'women's house' was established to assist women who have been caught in prostitution and drug addiction. The focal point in this area of care for women is one of welcome, hospitality and friendship. It is a case of establishing a good and ordinary relationship with the women. This approach has proved to be effective and invaluable for many women. There will be stories throughout this book about this sensitive and demanding ministry in which we come face to face with sadness and abuse, struggle and failure and hope and suffering.

Housing The Mission is responsible for three rooming houses at present—a group home, a block of flats and several individual flats around the St Kilda area. Through the housing ministry we have come to recognise just how important a stable home is for people with any form of addiction or illness.

Our first attempts at housing were in the parish terrace houses in Robe Street. There were three of them and when we took them over they had to be extensively renovated. We did this cheaply with live-in 'tradesmen' who were prepared to rough it a bit while they fixed the houses. The work took a long time because most of these men had a battle on their hands with alcohol. For some men, living in these houses in those early days was the opportunity they needed to make a new start. They were assisted to either obtain their own flat or move to a rehabilitation centre. In those three houses we had our share of laughs and tears, success and drama and all that makes up any sort of community life. Through these early experiences we were able to gain an appreciation of how important housing is if people are to make new beginnings.

Hostel Sacred Heart Mission took responsibility for the management of a special accommodation house in November 1989. This was a recently renovated building with accommodation for twenty-nine people, beautifully appointed and directed towards people who could afford an expensive place of care. It was decided that we would rent this building and offer it to people who had only the pension. The executive committee knew that this decision would be at a high financial cost. We were right. The hostel cost the Mission around $150,000 over two years.

The move to acquire the hostel came after several failed attempts for other properties in the area. We wanted to be involved in this area of care. It has been a burden financially, but no-one regrets the decision. Our efforts have been recognised with the Government's decision to purchase the building for us. This takes away the financial concern and ensures ongoing care for the residents.

If nothing else, the hostel undertaking has vindicated the attitude of being prepared to take a risk in caring for people. At first I talked in terms of accommodating pension-only people in what would be considered 'luxury arrangements'. After a short time I changed this attitude and talked in terms of such accommodations being the 'norm' for our people—not a luxury.

Recreation The word 'recreation' comes from re-creation, which seems to imply that such recreational activities are life-giving activities. That's certainly been the case with our experience in St Kilda.

Various programs have been developed. There are sporting events which provide opportunities to play football, basketball, tennis, bowls, volleyball, badminton, indoor bowling, cricket and swimming. There are social events which offer the chance to visit places such as an art gallery, museum, zoo, theatre and movies. There have been picnics and camps arranged and even the opportunity for a bit of work. It's amazing how many opportunities for 're-creation' exist.

Health clinic In 1989 a couple of chiropractors wandered into the Mission and offered to provide a free service to our people. From a simple beginning of two people working from one of our parlours, there is now a wide-ranging clinic for five days a week in a separate house.

Other professionals offering their services to low-income people include physiotherapists, podiatrists, dermatologists, naturopaths, masseuses, hairdressers, homeopaths, psychologists and dentists. There is also a weekly meditation group at the clinic.

The Mission has made available a ten-room house which serves as the clinic and also employs a coordinator for this ministry. Another group of volunteers serve as receptionists.

A spirit of unity

All of these areas of Mission life could be placed under the heading of 'care'. In addition, there are the day-to-day activities of parish life which bring people together. Sacred Heart Mission is the welfare arm of the Sacred Heart Parish. Such things as the playgroup for young mothers and their children, the social events in the parish, the liturgical life of the parish, youth ministry and so on help to build the parish into a caring Christian community who share life together.

The documentary 'Bread & Blessing' represented the culmination at a point of time in a journey that I have shared with many people. When I showed the documentary to a group of priests, one of them remarked that I didn't appear to do much because, throughout the documentary, I was forever sitting on a bench at the front of the Mission. I do work, but the main thrust in the Mission over the past couple of years has been to make each activity stand somewhat independent. Delegation of responsibility and decision making has been granted more and more to the individual services provided by the Mission. One of the important and yet difficult tasks for me as a priest in the Church today is to be able to give complete delegation of responsibility in areas which rightfully belong to the lay people in our Church community. This surely is a challenge for both priests and the Church as a whole. In West St Kilda this dream of mine has become a reality in a positive way with a team of religious and lay people who are, or have been, involved full-time in the work of the Church in St Kilda.

The challenge continues

Over the years, as the works of the Mission have developed, the number and type of people working on the team has varied. But we have always tried to find ways of working well together. One of the constant factors over the years has been the question of finding new ways to meet the needs of the team at a particular time. Just when you seem to work out the ideal way of team meetings, situations change and needs differ, and the ideal has to be revised again. But over the years we have persevered and have managed to maintain a team spirit in the Mission.

None of us could ever have dreamed that the Mission would grow to what it is today. We need to continually remind ourselves of the simple beginnings in ministering to people.

PART 2

A priest called Smith

CHAPTER 3

Growing Up

My family

In 1976 I wrote to my Archbishop, Frank Little, about the
need to try a new form of pastoral approach in Yarraville. In
my letter I wrote that 'I am sure my own background has
much to do with my decision. I lived in North Melbourne in
very simple circumstances. I received the benefits of
education via scholarships which opened up possibilities of
work for me which in turn led me to the priesthood. I have
never forgotten where I have come from'.

If these beginnings were so important, then I must try to
share them with you. For North Melbourne was indeed a
great place to be born and grow up. North Melbourne, first
suburb out from the city centre, was an old, established,
working-class area. It was here that my grandparents on both
sides had raised families. It was here that my parents also
raised their family.

On my father's side, the Smith family, my grandmother
was a devout Catholic and a beautiful lady. She died when I
was only six, but I have many precious memories of her love.
My grandfather was not a Catholic and consequently the

seven children were not given a Catholic upbringing. They
were baptised Catholics, but that was the beginning and the
end of the faith question. Grandfather Smith was a carpenter
and wheelwright, but in the 1920s he began a greengrocer
business in North Melbourne. The fruit business stayed with
the family until 1954 when our family left North Melbourne.

On my mother's side, the Troy family, my grandfather was
a Catholic from Irish stock. Although he didn't 'wear out the
kneelers', links were still there, however frail. My
grandmother, who died in 1986 at the age of ninety-six, was
not a Catholic by birth. Grandfather Troy was something of a
farmer in the early years of marriage. Then they settled into
Melbourne where my grandfather became a marine dealer,
which is a classy word for the local bottle-o—the man who
collected the empty bottles and returned them to the glass
companies. They first settled at Collingwood and later moved
to North Melbourne.

My father was born and raised in North Melbourne,
attended the Boundary Road State School, and at age twelve
virtually left school. He began at the Brunswick Technical
School, but never bothered to go except for the occasional day
to keep himself on the roll. In fact, he started work at age
twelve. He worked for a year at a nail factory and then settled
into the fruit business with his father. Thirty years later he
was still selling fruit.

My mother began school at the Gold Street State School in
Collingwood and left at the age of thirteen to begin work.
Mum worked on the process line at Prestige, turning out
stockings; this was the only job Mum had. It was where she
made lifetime friends including my godmother. When she
was fourteen the family moved to North Melbourne. At
fifteen Mum left home and was boarding because of 'hassles'
with her father.

There has been no mention of faith or church in my parents' life, precisely because there had been no instruction or church involvement. At fourteen, Mum went to the convent to be instructed for Communion. Duly instructed, Mum made her first Communion, but it was an unmarked day at home as no one from the family was there for the occasion. It was very much a personal thing for my mother, with no support from home. When she returned to the convent from the church to parade in her first Communion dress, one of the sisters immediately said that she would now be able to begin her instruction for Confirmation. 'No, thank you', replied my mother who had finished with instruction for the time being. Thirty years later, this sacrament would come along.

Priests have heard many times the wide range of reasons why people give up attending Mass. For my mother the reason was simple. At fifteen, just in the Church for a little while and going it alone, she went to Confession. It took only the smell of alcohol on the priest's breath to make up her mind that she would not go into that church again. As she said to her mother, 'I don't have to put up with that smell. I have enough of it at home!' The reasoning may have been wrong, but the effect was real.

So two people met and decided to get married. My father was one of seven children, none of whom were brought up as Catholics. My mother was one of three children, none of whom were ever practical Catholics, although both her brothers had some education at Catholic schools. When it came to marriage and a church there was only one choice—St Michael's, North Melbourne—because after all, they are both Catholics! My parents were married in a Catholic church, the only ones to do so from their families.

On 24 January 1939 I entered into the world. When it came to baptising their children, my parents had no hesitation and it was back to St Michael's Church. I would consider myself to be a very special baby because of what it cost to have me baptised. My father had learned early how to gamble, and Sunday mornings were spent dog racing at the swamp. My father had good racing dogs, as did my godfather Ishie (real name Bert), but on this particular Sunday both men were out of luck at the races and finished up broke. With a good deal of begging and borrowing among their friends, they raised one pound, which was a lot of money to give to the priest in 1939. How thrilled and grateful they were upon leaving the church after my baptism to be told by my grandmother not to worry about fixing up the priest. She had already given him one pound. Not to worry! They had already paid the priest who was by then probably saying to himself that the Smiths must have plenty of money to give him two offerings!

Nearly two years later my sister Pat arrived. The war was on and my father was away for a few years. At this time we were in the fruit shop on Melrose Street, North Melbourne. This was to be our home until I was fifteen years old. Dad arrived home after the war and our family was together at the fruit shop. There were two small houses behind the shop. In one was our family of four, while the house next door accommodated my grandfather and Dad's three unmarried brothers.

Pat and I were sent to St Michael's parish school because my parents believed that if we were christened Catholic we should have a chance to learn about it. For my mother it was certainly because she did not want us to have to go through what she did in order to understand the Catholic faith. My parents never practised any religion in the sense of going to church, because they had not been really instructed, but they did their best to make sure we had a chance to find out about the Catholic faith.

There was plenty of contact with the Church even if my parents were not attending on Sundays. One priest, and in fact the only one to ever visit the shop, was Father Vin Arthur. He asked my mother why she was not going to Mass. Her reply was, 'I just don't have the time'. Father Arthur replied that his mother had raised many children and still managed to find time. My mother's reply was, 'Did she have a fruit shop?' Father Arthur was a good friend to my parents as he was to so many families in North Melbourne at the time. Later on, he was a good friend to me as a priest.

Having a truck brought my father into very real contact with the Church. On Fridays the truck carried the school children to football and basketball games. This was supposed to be a business deal. It was only after the first few years without being paid that it became a love job! But that's how it was in North Melbourne. You didn't worry about money. As my father would say, there was money around among the lot of you. Whoever had the money, perhaps gained from a win at the dogs, helped out his mates. The Annual Communion Breakfasts also gave business to the fruit shop. That too was another love job! What I am saying is very simple. I have a very generous father who loves to help people any way he can.

Living in North Melbourne

The truck was also used to take crowds of people from our area to the football matches on Saturday. Every second Saturday the truck would head off to some far-away ground with a load of supporters. Beforehand, people going to the football matches came to the shop to have lunch in our kitchen behind the shop. Lunch was an enormous pot of soup, a stack of bread and butter and a large tray of cream cakes which Dad would buy each Saturday. Nobody bothered to count heads.

If there was food left in the kitchen, you were welcome to have it. People were very much at home behind the shop.

What made North Melbourne a good place to live was people. People were tough in North Melbourne, but so was life for many of them. In North people were sociable and helped each other. They were battlers. People knew each other. Summer brought families out into the streets. The adults would sit and yarn on the nature strips that divided the roads. The children would play marbles, football or a thousand and one other games on those summer nights. On some nights fifty or sixty children of all ages would be playing together in the street. Growing up with so many friends around was healthy.

There were nature strips and triangles because the houses had no spare space. There were very few houses with front gardens as most were built on to the street. Only a few had sideways between them because they were built terrace style, one onto the other. And the backyards were small. Space in the houses of North Melbourne was very limited so the people met in the street.

Gambling, like the neighborhood pubs, was part and parcel of daily life for many families. The bookmaker operating up the back lane was a way of life. Police raids were not too successful because of the 'nit' system of men keeping watch on the various corners. When they did manage to reach the bookmaker, it was a mad helter-skelter up the many lanes, with people jumping into backyards. Once in the backyards, they were safe from the police. Such betting was illegal but honest. I can vouch for that because I used to help work out the bets for my father who was the bookmaker for awhile!

Life could be boring as punters waited for the next race to start, so the great Australian sport of 'two-up' was always a feature up the lanes near the bookmaker, and on Sundays at selected spots.

Growing up in North helped to fashion me and the values I was to live by.

Our home

Stories I recall about North Melbourne centre on the houses and the conditions in which people lived as well as my homelife. Dampness, rats, overcrowding, were all taken for granted. Dampness meant that the floorboards would every so often give up the struggle. People falling through a rotted board was nothing unusual. When my auntie fell through a whole section which gave way, that was more serious!

People fixed their own houses. I remember my Uncle Herbie fixing the ceiling from inside the roof. He missed his step on the roof beams and stepped on the ceiling itself and fell through the ceiling. It wouldn't have mattered so much, but the dinner had been served and lay ready on the kitchen table.

At home, I could always bring friends for a meal with virtually no notice. This would be handled with ease. Anyone was welcome at any time, even without warning.

If people lacked the 'good things' of this life there was plenty of laughter and happiness. By the descriptions given in the books which I read in seminary, I would classify our home as part of a slum, like many houses in North Melbourne. What I remember is that it was a friendly place where people knew each other and cared about each other. It was a place where people helped each other if they could.

My parents may not have been church-going Catholics, but they were certainly practical Christians. Friendliness, hospitality, generosity, sharing and struggling, were some of the lessons I learned by growing up in a place such as North Melbourne.

Beginnings are important and I am very proud of my beginnings. My parents and my grandparents I speak of with pride. The values instilled into me, not by words but by example, are always with me. My yearning to return to these beginnings brought this story to its starting point.

CHAPTER 4

The Way to Priesthood

In 1968, a few months before I was ordained, I met a mate from my YCW days in Ascot Vale. Not having seen me for a few years, Phil asked what I was doing. I pointed to the seminary up the hill and simply said that I was up there now. Phil asked quite seriously, 'What sort of job?' With the reply that I was a student, he burst into spontaneous laughter.

Phil laughed because the thought of my becoming a priest would never have entered his mind. It had never entered my mind either, until a few months before I went to the seminary. However, ordinations and priests don't just happen. They are the result of being called, and the call is individual. I am grateful to many people along life's way who helped me, perhaps unknowingly, to discover this call to priesthood. People, moments and opportunities opened new horizons for me on the path to becoming a priest.

Schooling

Education gave me a big opportunity. Through scholarships I was able to go on to secondary education. I had chances denied to so many of my friends. Without scholarships, I probably would have left school at fourteen or fifteen to begin work. My sister Pat left school the day that she turned fourteen in November, not even waiting for final tests! This would have been the way for most of the young people growing up with me in North Melbourne. Instead I was able to go on to matriculation (Year 12) in 1955 and then off into the work force with opportunities abounding.

Along with the knowledge gained through education there was the influence and friendships of some of the brothers who taught me in these secondary school years. The example and influence of 'Charlie' Harrison was more important than I realised at the time.

Brother Harrison taught me for only one year (Year 8) at St Peter's School in West Melbourne. This was a unique type of school in the Catholic education system. It drew students from several parish schools to study for the Government scholarship. After this year the students went off to various secondary colleges—I went to St Joseph's in North Melbourne. This was one of the great fun years for me as we learned far more than was needed to earn a scholarship. Sport, music, games and even dancing were on the programme during this one year.

There were forty of us in that '51 class and I would be confident in saying that Brother Harrison touched each one of us, our families too, in a special way. An example of this respect was a reunion party at our home in 1960 when this group of twenty-one year olds were all waiting to see Brother Harrison before we had a drink. He was coming to our home for an evening with a couple of the 'boys', but we had arranged a surprise party for him. However, because he knew that there were only a few close friends, he didn't worry about being late . . . very late. It was a hot night, but none of us even took off our jackets and ties until he came. It turned out to be a great night.

'Charlie' went to Sydney in 1952, the year after teaching us, and a few years later went to India where he has been teaching since. This brother, in one year, made a lifetime impression upon me. It was a thrill to spend a week with him at a college at Bajpe, near Mangalore, in the south of India while I was overseas in 1979. To be able to share something of his life's work with Indian children was a rich experience for me. I again had the chance to stay with him in India during 1991, this time at an orphanage in Calcutta. Although he has been away from me for most of the time since that one year in 1951, his role in my call is important. He is one of many people along the way to my ordination.

At St Joseph's College in North Melbourne, run by the Christian Brothers, I also made lifetime friends with other young students and some of the brothers. Brother O'Donnell—'Bill' or 'Silvertop'—is one of those fellows who somehow manages to keep up with his students even after thirty-five years. I guess that for these men, the students were their life. They gave total commitment to their call and their work. 'Old Bill' certainly fell into that category.

Brother O'Donnell also helped me after leaving school. For five years I ploughed away at my studies in accountancy. I was off to a flying start in my first year of work in 1956. I passed a couple of exams immediately. However, over the next few years, accountancy at night school became more of a burden than a planning for the future. Consequently, I was not the best student.

I was fortunate that I did my studies at the Christian Brothers College North Melbourne night school, and that I had a good friend in Brother O'Donnell. This helped because he did not bother to send me accounts for various terms which I would start and never complete. However, I did manage to learn a fair bit of the principles of accounting which have certainly stood me in good stead.

Work and YCW

From secondary school it was off to work in 1956 in the field of accountancy. A year in the office of a chartered accountant in the city was long enough to know that this was not my niche. The opportunity to work in the office of a wholesale hardware firm came along; so I began a job that was to give me plenty of experience and, again, lifetime friends. For a little over three years I worked at Lords Hardware in a job which could have had great possibilities for me because of the broad experience that was given to me by my boss. This didn't eventuate because of an offer to work full-time with the Young Christian Workers Movement, the YCW.

Of all the factors that influenced my life, the YCW was the most significant. My association with the YCW began when I left school and joined the YCW football team at Ascot Vale. Football was one of my loves so I had to find a team. With another lad from North Melbourne, Albert Stuckey, I wandered along to the training night with the football club and started attending the YCW meetings on Friday nights.

Football was the attraction, and at the meetings I found a new group of friends and so became part of the gang. For more than a year, the YCW meant football, picnics, dances and a full social life. Albert had taken me along, but he didn't stay. I did stay and from this, so many things would derive.

During this time I certainly made some lifetime friends. Although in the early sixties we drifted apart, we had a reunion gathering shortly before I was ordained at the end of 1967. It was a night to celebrate the fact that I was now wearing a clerical collar and approaching the priesthood ordination. Out came all the old 50's records and we danced and had a great night reliving all those old songs. This group has continued to meet over the years and, particularly because of these early shared times, has been important to my priesthood.

In 1957 Father John Fraser, who was the assistant priest at Ascot Vale, called me aside and told me that he was starting a leaders' group and that he wanted me to be part of it. I didn't know what a leaders' group was and Father Fraser was not about to tell me. 'Come to the meeting and find out' was the extent of his information and there wasn't really a great deal of choice about whether I went. So I accepted his 'invitation' and attended the meeting.

I remember my preparation for that meeting. Knowing that it was something to do with the Church, the Mass must be part of it. Out came the old missal. With the help of the calendar I worked out which Sunday we had just passed. I read the Gospel for the previous Sunday and also studied the parts of the Mass. There was no way that I would be caught out by Father Fraser. I was ready for any questions.

The YCW introduced me to a whole new approach to life. The YCW is a youth organisation founded by Joseph Cardijn, a Belgian priest, which had spread around the world. It was an organisation based on formation of leaders, young people who would be apostles in their daily lives at work, at home and at play. The mission of the YCW leader was to be found very simply in one's daily life. For the next three years I was in the leaders' group at Ascot Vale, learning about life and about myself through the YCW method of formation.

In this program, the Enquiry method asked questions about life and moved to discussion of the facts which we as a group were asked to find out and share. The secret of the Enquiry method was that it started from life and not from guesses or book facts. The Gospel discussions introduced me to the person and the teaching of Jesus. Again, not in an abstract intellectual way but as related to our enquiries and our life. Jesus was presented as having something to say about my daily life and my involvement with people wherever I might meet them. Through personal discovery about Jesus, we were learning about our life, our mission to others and about the dignity of all people. But the learning had to be translated into action. One of the key factors in YCW was 'formation through action'.

My understanding and my involvement in the Ascot Vale YCW changed very much through this period of growth in the leaders' group. In 1959 I became the president of the YCW in Ascot Vale and also became involved in diocesan meetings. To the annoyance of Brother O'Donnell, who was in charge of the accountancy night school at North Melbourne, YCW continually interfered with my accountancy studies. It seemed to me that accountancy could be picked up later, but the YCW work couldn't wait.

Full-time work with the YCW At the end of 1959 I was asked to work full-time for the YCW as Diocesan Secretary for Melbourne. I was being asked to give up an excellent job with a good salary in order to work for the YCW with a wage barely enough to manage on. I went straight home and told my parents and the next day gave notice of leaving my job. Looking back I am amazed that I was able to accept this job with such ease and spontaneity. I guess that I was so involved with the YCW that other matters such as job security or study didn't rate very high.

This was one of those important life-decisions which you make without realising how much it will affect your future. Here I worked with other full-timers such as Jim Wilson, Jim Ross, Brian Hayes and Bert De Luca, all of whom were dedicated to the YCW. Each of these people had an impact on my life during the next year.

I must single out one person and that is the chaplain, Father Kevin Toomey. His energy and dedication influenced me; his talks with me and concern for me challenged me and eventually brought me to the priesthood.

Father Toomey was chaplain of the YCW for many years. In that time he had a profound impact on the lives of many young people in the YCW, as well as many young people in trouble for whatever reason. He was tireless in work for youth and conveyed his enthusiasm, zeal and dedication to thousands of leaders at training weekends. We would joke about the way the froth would be on his lips as he exhorted us at these weekends, but we were sold by his commitment. There seemed to be no limit to the hours he would spend with young people. He always seemed to be able to lift himself even when he was tired.

My work with the YCW involved me in a constant round of parish meetings and training weekends for leaders. During the day there were so many young people visiting the office—sometimes with a worry and often just for a chat. Life was very busy throughout this time. Often I would be at the office at 7.00 a.m. to get some urgent work completed because the days were so full. With men such as Father Toomey and the lay people—Jim, Brian and Bert—the life of a full-time YCW worker was full, busy and very happy.

Overseas experience In mid-1960 I was nominated by the YCW to attend a conference of the World Assembly of Youth in Africa. I did not build up my hopes because there were more experienced applicants, but the nomination was in. I could hardly believe it when I arrived home from a meeting one night and was told by my mother that I had been selected by the National Youth Council to attend the conference. The next few weeks were very hectic, getting organised with passport, travel arrangements and injections. At the end of July I headed off on a trip that was to change my life completely.

There were two others besides me chosen to represent Australia at this conference. Peter Wilenski from Sydney, was the nomination of the National Union of Australian University Students and Harold Jenner, was the National President of the YMCA. Harold took ill just before the conference and was replaced by Betty King, also of the YCW. The conference was in Ghana and brought together almost 400 people from ninety-two countries. I found myself one of the youngest delegates at the conference among so many 'experts'. The conference exposed me to an experience of other cultures, religions and values. It also forced me to think about issues of a global nature, particularly regarding injustice and oppression of working people throughout the world.

Many of the papers delivered at the conference may have been over my head at the time, but for a month I was able to share ideas, experiences and friendship with people from many countries. At the conference there were YCW people from more than a dozen countries and a couple of the YCW international executive members. Contact with these YCW people was beneficial. Among them were two young men who could not go back to their countries. One was from Cuba and one from the Congo; both were in trouble in their own countries because they were YCW full-time workers. I certainly felt small-time against such people as these young men.

The conference was for one month, but the YCW arranged for me to be away for almost four months to have the chance to visit Johannesburg in South Africa and Lagos in Nigeria on the way to the conference, as well as several countries in Europe and Asia on the way home.

There were both good and hurtful experiences. It was an unpleasant shock in Johannesburg to see first-hand the black-white question and the effects of the apartheid policy. I was staying with Eric Tyacke, a YCW worker who had gone to Johannesburg to help develop the YCW. He was working under extreme difficulties. Many years later I read of his 'house arrest' and ultimate expulsion from South Africa. It's not necessarily pleasant, but it is very formative to be with such men even for a few days.

Another 'unpleasant' experience was being by myself in Lagos. Here I was staying in a luxurious hotel while outside the door were the worst slums I had ever seen, although there were far worse sights awaiting me in India later in the trip. In Lagos, confronted by the poverty and really alone, I shed tears of homesickness and would have liked to return home right at that moment.

After leaving the conference I spent time in several countries with YCW people and attended many meetings. I enjoyed the hospitality of the YCW in England, Belgium, France, Pakistan, India, Ceylon and Singapore. Without thinking about it, I was experiencing the richness of an international movement. In other places, such as Lourdes, Liseaux, Rome and Jerusalem, the experiences were of a spiritual nature and were helping me in a different way.

There was the business side of the trip in England, visiting the YCW centres in Coventry, Manchester and Middlesbrough. I was being feted as an expert international visitor, but in fact I was learning all the time. I was staying with the full-time workers in London, at the home of Patrick Keegan, the first international president of the YCW. I also had the chance to take in the sights of London. This in itself was a great education.

I spent three days at the international headquarters of the YCW in Brussels. In both England and Brussels I was with YCW people who all shared their dedication and commitment with me. Imagine the feelings I had when I spent three mornings with Joseph Cardijn, who had founded the YCW, in Brussels, serving his morning Mass and having breakfast together—just the two of us.

This was a time that would remain with me and an experience for which I will be forever grateful. He talked with me about my family, my work, my people, my hopes. He was the first to talk with me about a possible vocation. That such an international figure, with so many pressing matters to concern him, could take such a personal interest in me over these three mornings was an experience and a lesson for life.

Then it was on to Paris and the YCW, but with a problem because I couldn't speak French. Here began a 'spiritual trip' because in successive stops I visited Liseaux, Nevers, Lourdes, Rome and Jerusalem. In Liseaux, I 'met' St Therese through reading a book about her life and her way, visiting the convent and seeing the reminders of her life. At Nevers I saw the incorrupt body of St Bernadette and spent a quiet couple of hours in meditation and prayer. On then to Lourdes, there I spent three days alone, including the last night in a vigil of prayer. This was all a new experience for me.

Rome included an audience with Pope John XXIII in a large room, where I felt that he was talking to me alone and not to the couple of thousand people present. It was at this time that I wrote home to Father Toomey about my thoughts of a vocation. I had to wait over two weeks for his reply which could be summed up as, 'Have a good time, and we'll talk about it when you get home'.

After Rome I intended to go to Jerusalem for a day. A priest in Rome told me to make it three days. Eventually I stayed there for two weeks. I boarded the plane in Rome for Tel Aviv and arrived at midnight without accommodation. I went by hire car to Jerusalem with a group of tourists.

When we pulled up at the plush King David Hotel I had a few worries until I saw the YMCA sign across the road from the hotel. At 2.00 a.m. I found myself in the YMCA demanding a room from an irate porter who did not speak much English. When he realised that I was going to camp for the night in the lobby, he managed to find a bed for me sharing a room. This is when providence took over!

As I was filling in the register, I saw that the name of the person with whom I would be sharing was Ken Heslin, from New Zealand, who had been at Ghana with me. When last seen, two months earlier, he had been heading home to New Zealand. I had the greatest delight waking Ken and we danced around that room.

Ken and I spent a couple of weeks together in the Holy Land, sharing many rich spiritual moments together. Our visits to the numerous sacred sites around Jerusalem and trips to Bethlehem, Hebron, Jericho and so on, added fuel to the fire as far as my thoughts about vocation. They were valuable experiences and enriched by being able to share them with Ken.

We then went together to Karachi. Again I experienced the hospitality of YCW people. The most vivid experiences were our visits to a leper colony and a slum village area. The repulsion I first felt at walking among lepers is with me even now as I write. The abject poverty of these lepers and the people in the slum village evoked feelings of utter helplessness. In India I was to see the same poverty, and such experiences constantly challenged my values.

In Bombay I attended the National Conference of the Indian YCW and met delegates from the main Indian centres. Dedicated priests and laity from all over India gave me an enriching experience and the opportunity to reflect on the role of the YCW in Australia. From Bombay I went to Bangalore to see priests and government people about the possibility of introducing the YCW. Then on to Madras where I stayed with Father Thomas Joseph, the chaplain, and had the chance to make a short retreat with YCW leaders.

Finally on to Ceylon and Singapore. I spent a few days in each place with the YCW leaders. By this time my heart was ahead of me and I was ready to get back home. I met and stayed with wonderful people, in particular great men like Rene Delacluse, Rienze Rupasinghe and Arul Nathan. Rene was French and had been working to develop the YCW in Southeast Asia, Rienze was from Ceylon and was the key local YCW person for the area, Arul was the president of the Singapore YCW. All of these men have made contributions to the church and world in so many ways then and later.

On the trip overseas I had been given the chance not only to meet many people and to have many experiences, but more important, I had been given the chance to look at my life away from the demands and the people in my life in Melbourne.

Through this whole YCW process I had come to an awareness of my own importance and my own call. From the prospective leader studying his missal so as not to be caught I had moved from discovery of Jesus Christ in the Gospel discussions, to a life of prayer and sacraments, stemming from and related to my daily life with people in the YCW. These experiences along with a whole set of values and ideals instilled in me by my family and my schooling, had now brought me to the priesthood.

To the seminary

I found myself to be something of a celebrity on my return home. Slide shows and guest appearances were in demand. However, my main pre-occupation was the decision to become a priest. This became definite by the end of the year, but I still had a few hurdles to get over because, although I had the necessary standard of education, I did not have Latin (Year 11) among my subjects. I would need to wait a year and study Latin before I would be accepted in the seminary. I made it clear to Father Toomey that they could have me now or not at all, and that another year could see me married. The regulations were bent a little and a deal worked out. I studied Latin for about six weeks with Gary Eastman, a YCW leader, and sat for a little exam set by the seminary authorities, and passed. I was accepted to enter the seminary in March 1961.

This episode with Latin was something like my past catching up with me. At the end of Year 10 we had been given our first choice of subjects and we could do either Latin or history. I chose history. However, Brother Crowle said there were no choices for me and that I could do both. I insisted there was a choice but still had to do both. For that whole year I did no homework in Latin and no study whatever. I knew that I would not need it, or so I thought. When it came to the end of the year and time to sit for the public examinations, Brother Crowle refused to sign my form and that of a few others, unless we all sat for Latin. I can recall saying to Brother Crowle that it was a waste of my parents' money because I could not pass the exam as I had not studied for it. His reply was that he was not the one wasting but that I was. So I had to sit for Latin. At the end of the required minimum thirty minutes at the exam, I stood up and handed in a blank sheet of paper with my examination number on it. Of course I felt like the big hero doing this but, six years later, I found myself struggling to get into the seminary because of this escapade.

I managed to pass the little exam set by the cathedral anyway. I was given the questions to take home, and I stayed at home to do this all-important exam. Without making a full confession, I reckon that if I had failed that exam under these arrangements, I would have been rejected for lack of initiative. I can confess to making a few deliberate mistakes to give the right impression of someone having a 'fair dinkum' go at the exam! The main thing was I passed and that meant that I was in.

When I told my parents about my possible decision, I received tremendous support. They certainly were not surprised. However, I remember having a big argument with my mother in the months before entering seminary. She wanted to know if I was really sure about this question of not getting married, and I told her that she didn't know what she was talking about. Words to that effect anyway.

Later on in the seminary, I wrote a letter to my parents acknowledging that Mum knew me far better than I knew myself. This celibacy thing was already proving very difficult I believe that Mum knew just how much I needed to love someone and to be loved in return. And this was only my first year of study!

CHAPTER 5

A Twenty-five Year Journey

Seminary years

After eight years of study and formation in the seminary I made it to my ordination as a priest on 15 June 1968. The period in the seminary sometimes seemed so long; on two particular occasions I virtually packed my bags. Some of the study seemed so useless, some of the rules irrelevant and some of the tasks so annoying. At times I wondered what all this had to do with my becoming a priest. There were also the good times and the many bonds of friendship established.

I remember sitting in the garden at Werribee during one of the very early retreats. With my accountancy background I carefully worked out how many hours of retreat, prayer and recollection would be involved in eight years and whether I could put up with it! What a horrible thought when I realised that it wouldn't be only for these eight years, but that this was part of the priest's life. Over the time in the seminary all these moments helped bring me to ordination.

Dramatic changes were taking place in the life of the seminary between 1961 and 1968. The way of life into which I had entered in 1961 was vastly different to that from which I left in 1968. The Vatican Council had taken place, change was sweeping through the Church and had touched seminary life. Several new initiatives were introduced into the seminary in the latter part of my seminary training. It really was quite an exciting period in the life of the Church. It could be a bit confusing though just the same. One example I recall was our study of 'Theology of the Church'. In 1965 we had Father Jackie Meagher teaching us, and he was quite a character to say the least. During this year he spent most of our class time haranguing a particular book called *Apologetics and the Biblical Christ* by Father Avery Dulles. Next year, Father Peter Little taught this subject and this was his text book!

Somewhere in those years, a new initiative was brought in. We were allowed one day per month away from the seminary for pastoral experience. This was a major breakthrough at the time, although it would seem insignificant for students now. Some of those pastoral experience days, left to your own discretion, were quite innovative. One of the most interesting of these days was a visit to the city morgue and being shown through the premises which would not be everybody's idea of a day out.

During these years in the seminary, I had the opportunity to take on a different job each year over the Christmas holidays. I decided I would use this opportunity to gain new experiences. One year I worked in a factory, another year as a ward assistant at a psychiatric hospital and another as a ward assistant at an institution for intellectually disabled children. I had a go at sorting mail at a post office, organising holiday camps for migrant children and twice going off to New Guinea to work at a mission station. Each one of these experiences introduced me to another aspect of life and all added something more to my training and understanding of people and their needs.

At the end of my seventh year, I went back to A.A. Lords Ltd in Flemington where I had previously worked. It was great to go back to the same place to meet people with whom I had worked and to experience their support. When I arrived at Lords to make arrangements, dressed in clerical suit, I went out to the store where I was greeted by George Boyce who said among other things, 'I reckon you'll make a great ***** priest'. This was really a great welcome home.

Ordination

It was 15 June and my ordination day arrived. I was a priest. In the days when rubrics, the Church rules for ceremonies, were so important, I have little recollection of my ordination in the cathedral. Too much was going on and we had to remember where to stand, how to stand, and so on. I really didn't absorb all that was happening around me.

On the afternoon of my ordination I headed off with the men of the family—Dad, brother-in-law Don, and Uncle Tom—to a football match. At home, we had been just sitting around. That night, we went to Ascot Vale for benediction, and the next day to West Brunswick for the celebration of my first Mass. Now the realisation was hitting me between the eyes. I was among so many people whom I had known and loved on the way to becoming a priest. There were so many faces in front of me in the packed church at West Brunswick. These were the people who meant so much to me.

As Father Toomey preached at my first Mass, and again at the hall afterwards as Father Fraser spoke about me, I was so aware of how blessed I had been with family, friends, experiences and opportunities. As I spoke to the crowd of people in the hall, my eyes were filled and my voice gave way as I saw all these people who had loved me on the way to becoming a priest. I found that speech to be one of the hardest that I have ever given.

While I was in seminary, my parents had taken instruction in the Church. At the end of 1961 they had been confirmed after receiving the sacraments of both Confession and Eucharist. My grandparents had returned to the Church in 1963 and my grandfather had died with all the sacraments. I was so aware of these and other moments as I stood before the people. The following Sunday I returned to Ascot Vale and offered Mass for the people in the parish which had helped me so much.

There were a few anxious times waiting for the news about our first appointments. When I received mine I was very happy because I was going to Sandringham. It wasn't the place, but the fact that my boss would be Father John Kelly, who later became a Bishop.

Each priest or religious person has his or her own story. Each story is unique. In that sense, mine is nothing special. Our experiences stay with us and make us what we are, and what we are is our greatest gift.

Sandringham

Sandringham is down the beach way. That was about all I knew. In fact I had to find my way to the church with a street directory on the seat beside me. Even so, I had to stop twice to get my bearings. Finally I pulled in to a service station and an attendant directed me 200 yards around the corner. A great start! On arrival I found Father Kelly in overalls after a working bee.

My first Mass in this parish was celebrated with wooden boxes covering holes in the floor and temporary stands for a lectern. This was because renovations of the old church were well underway. Because of these renovations I can well remember my first morning at Sacred Heart Church. The platform for the altar was being rebuilt, and I had to be careful around the altar. My big moment during this first morning with the people of Sandringham came when I went to preach at the temporary lectern. As is my custom, I placed my hands firmly on the lectern and leaned on them. Unfortunately the lecture top which held sundry books, bits of paper for notices (this was before the days of parish newsletters) and assorted other items, immediately flipped in the opposite direction and sent all the papers flying. It was a good way to let people know that I had arrived.

In the old Sacred Heart Church in Sandringham there were to be many memorable moments. On one occasion, during a heavy bout of rain, the water came in from a blocked drain at the side of the church and straight across the floor in front of the sanctuary. I had to interrupt my sermon while one of the parishioners, Dr John Wright-Smith, with the assistance of the altar servers, removed their shoes and socks, rolled up their trousers, and proceeded to push the water back out into the yard. This happened between the pulpit and the front seats and was rather a distraction. It was made worse when one of the servers, Shaun Carey, slipped and fell into the water. Stories such as these could be recounted one after the other.

I was in this parish for over three years, with two parish priests, both of whom helped me in many ways and became good friends of mine. With Father Kelly I enjoyed two years of ministry in a happy atmosphere. Father John Scarborough came then and we also had a good year together. The presbytery at Sandringham was an old house and Father Kelly loved to have people around, so the doors were always open. Father Scarborough was not quite accustomed to the style of house which the Kelly-Smith regime had been operating. He 'spent the first six months trying to keep out of my way and the second six months trying to keep up with me'. These were his words at the blessing of the new church some years later.

There were good times with the young people in Sandringham. They were times that also involved the rest of the parish. For example, a concert was staged at the local community hall. It was a night which involved many groups of people, but was staged by the initiative of the young people. I made my serious debut as an actor on that night, playing Lucy, the mill girl, in *A Fruity Melodrama*. The hall was packed and, twenty years later, people still recall that concert.

There was an old school building which had been condemned, but which the young people took over as their clubroom. It was in need of some repair and particularly needed painting. I said they could paint it any colour they wanted. When I walked in later I was greeted by walls, doors, windows and ceiling all painted the one colour—black! It was unbelievable. However, when they had various dances and functions at night, and with the appropriate decorations, it really did look fantastic.

On another occasion, a group of young people asked if they could decorate the church for Christmas to celebrate the birthday of Christ and make it look like a birthday party. When they finished decorating there were streamers and Christmas bunting everywhere, golden twisting tinsel dangling on the wall behind the altar, the tabernacle highlighted by a spotlight, and an enormous twisting ball above the main altar also highlighted by a spotlight. It was something of a shock to the system at first when you walked into the church, but people appreciated the effort of the young people.

At the end of 1970 I organised a trip to New Guinea. Twelve of us went to a place called Sissano on the northern coast. Our task was to build a school, and we planned for it over several months. There were fundraising events, collecting of gear to take with us and so forth.

One of the fundraising efforts for this trip was a chook killing day. I purchased 400 chooks from the seminary and we killed them in the Gadsdens' backyard in Sandringham. Over two weekends we sold the chooks outside the church and the profits went towards the New Guinea trip. Again, the young people were involved in this exercise. On this day some killed, some plucked, some gathered feathers, some dug holes, while others prepared the cups of tea. Depending on their aptitude for blood and guts, they could find a suitable job. We repeated the exercise the following year but, maybe because of the quality of the chooks, we had trouble getting rid of all the chooks this time. Funny thing about that!

It's one of those worn-out sayings that the first parish is the one that you love the most. All I know is that I was lucky to be with two parish priests who were both enthusiastic, each in their own way, and who both enjoyed having people around the presbytery. Both gave me complete freedom to work in my own way and encouraged me in my efforts. The people of Sandringham gave their priests tremendous support and in those three years I was able to be part of many new undertakings. They were enjoyable and formative years.

Glenhuntly

Then on to Glenhuntly to work with an elderly priest, Father Patrick Gleeson, who was more than happy, in his words, to 'give the horse plenty of rein'. Because of poor health, in the form of arthritis, 'Old Paddy' was unable to get around himself. But he was pleased to let things happen. He knew the people and had a wealth of knowledge and experience from which I certainly gained.

Here I was given the chance to experiment in liturgy, parish council programmes, youth work and many other areas. I was living in an old house that had served as a presbytery for many years, and again, it was an open house.

Father Paddy Gleeson had been, throughout his priesthood, very dedicated to both visitation and preaching. At this time he was almost fifty years ordained and unable to visit. But when I arrived and started visiting, he actually got his walking stick and hat and tried to have a go again. It was too much for him in his state of health, but at least he wanted to try. He was a man who did not like having a fuss made of him and so in all of his priesthood had never had a farewell from any parish. When his golden jubilee was approaching in 1974, he arranged to have a holiday home to Ireland so that he would not be around at the time and no fuss could be made.

Aware of this, I arranged for Paddy to attend a senate of priests meeting in our area just before he left, which was in fact a surprise celebration for his fiftieth anniversary. After Bishop Kelly had spoken about him, his reply could be summed up with his remark that 'It's nice to hear your panegyric before you die'. On his return from Ireland, I had arranged a 'welcome home' evening in the parish hall which was to be combined with a presentation and recognition of his fifty years of priesthood. We disguised this in the form of a parish get-together. Unfortunately, some of the priests invited to this function went to the presbytery beforehand and enjoyed a drink with Paddy who was in no great hurry to go across to the hall because it was only a parish get-together. In fact we had the hall packed with people sitting in rows and rows of seats with nothing to do except wait for his arrival. It was forty-five minutes late when we eventually managed to get Paddy to come across to the gathering. It was a great night and this old priest stood on the stage, unable to respond because of his emotional state, it was a moment to remember for all of us in Glenhuntly at that time. Paddy had spent twenty years in that parish and this was a recognition of his work.

Father Gleeson enjoyed having people around so a happy atmosphere prevailed in the presbytery during those years. In this parish I was responsible for administration, financial and building ventures with the support and approval of Father Gleeson. If the years at Sandringham had been informative, then I suppose these years could be seen as a time for experimenting, particularly with lay people.

During these three years I had also been diocesan chaplain of the Young Christian Students group (YCS). These were difficult years for the various organisations in Catholic action. After eighteen months as chaplain, the organisation had virtually collapsed to a handful of groups and the executive was faced with the task of rebuilding the YCS with some new model for the future.

I was involved with the Senate of Priests for two years in Glenhuntly. We attempted some new levels of co-operation between priests and religious persons working in seven neighbouring parishes of which Glenhuntly was one. The religious personnel in those seven parishes amounted to about 180 people, serving in schools, hospitals, parishes, places of prayer and so on. Some interesting small achievements took place in those couple of years with this group.

Again, as at Sandringham, a lot of effort went into my work with young people with the YCW. We staged concerts each year and also arranged trips to New Guinea. At the end of 1973 there was a request for four young people to go to a mission station in New Guinea on fairly short notice. I approached four young people after Mass on a Sunday; during that afternoon the four of them all agreed to go and were planning to leave in a couple of weeks. It was an on-the-spot decision by them. The deal was that if they could go, we would have functions after Christmas to cover half the cost of their fare. However, on their return, none of the four wanted their half of the expenses. They felt they had been the ones who had gained from the experience.

The following year, at the end of 1974, a group of twelve young people went off to Mendi diocese in New Guinea, to work at various stations. There were activities to help subsidise some of the young people and to buy a few things for the missions. Again, the young people learned the art of killing chooks. I have no doubt that these trips to New Guinea were invaluable experiences for each of the young people who went. It also contributed a great amount to the life of the priests and religious persons on the mission stations.

Do circumstances just happen? Here I was, having served in two parishes, and in both places I had lived in an old house which was an open house to people. In both parishes new presbyteries were built after my departure. By their design they were not meant to be open-style presbyteries. It would not, and in fact could not, have been quite the same. These two old houses had given me extra advantages at least for my way of working and thinking about ministry.

A difficult time

Looking back over my six years at Sandringham and Glenhuntly, it was a great time of learning and growth. I worked with fine people in both parishes and established life-long supportive contact with many of them. That was the external side of me, but my internal reflection on this period of my life was intense loneliness. I struggled, particularly in the area of celibacy. I could easily quote the standard reasons for this—living situation, lack of someone to share my work with, frustration, overwork and tiredness and a host of other reasons. The continuing struggle with celibacy focused particularly on the desire for a family of my own.

It would probably come as a surprise to people who knew me during those years, to learn that on three occasions I was close to leaving the priesthood. In fact after just one year of ministry as a priest, I had contacted a priest friend of mine to say that I'd had enough. Somehow or other I managed to hang in basically because of this belief of a call which I could not shake off.

Sometime during 1971, I had a yarn with Bishop Kelly about how well I wasn't going. He told me that my trouble was that I had not learned to live with loneliness. I agreed with him that I may not have learned to live alone, but that loneliness was an evil in the world. I certainly didn't want to live with loneliness.

Towards the end of my time at Glenhuntly I approached Archbishop Little with a few of my thoughts about ministry. I felt that I could boast a good record at both Sandringham and Glenhuntly. In both places I had been free to work with people in my own way and there had been good results to show for my efforts. What I tried to convey to him was a certain discontent within me. I wanted to return to the inner-city area. I even expressed to the archbishop that I would feel like turning down any appointment to an outer suburban parish to show how strongly I felt about this.

There were five requests that I made when I visited the archbishop. When the appointments came out, none of these five requests had been granted. When I heard that I was appointed to Macleod just prior to Christmas 1974, my first reaction was one of anger. I would simply refuse to go to Macleod. However, after a few weeks and with advice from a couple of priest friends, I took up the appointment. The main reason for my discontent was the fact that I had not been listened to and had been given exactly the opposite of what I requested. I felt I was being tested.

The living situation which I encountered at Macleod was vastly different to that of both Sandringham and Glenhuntly. I did endeavour to tackle this new appointment positively, but within a few days difficulties arose regarding both the areas of my work and the manner in which I would be able to work. I decided that I could not live out my priesthood in the way that would be expected of me. After five weeks at Macleod parish, I was sent to 'plug a hole' at Box Hill for two weeks because the priest had left the parish without notice.

It's rather ironic that at Macleod and Box Hill, I was sent to take the place of a priest who had made a decision to leave the priesthood. At that particular time I myself was struggling to hold on to my priesthood. God must have a good sense of humour!

During these weeks I had meetings with the archbishop to convey my disappointment at not being heard. We had to resolve our communication difficulty. While at Box Hill, I was asked to take up an appointment to Yarraville parish. After a couple of months at Yarraville, I found myself under the care of my doctor John Wright-Smith. He was treating me for depression caused by anxiety and exhaustion. He even made me promise to take some medication for a short time. I did this, although I refused to accept his diagnosis of depression. Later on in the year, after a good holiday and some months at Yarraville, I realised how down I had been.

Through these months of being down, I remember one very direct form of consultation with Dr John Wright-Smith. After chatting with me for awhile, he asked me three questions in rapid fire. The questions, to the best of my memory were, 'Do you have a relationship with a woman? Are you in love with her? Do you want to leave the priesthood?' I answered, also in rapid fire, 'Yes. Yes. No.' John's response was 'Okay. Well, let's start dealing with one thing at a time'. Details about the situation are not necessary but I attained a greater appreciation of my priesthood, myself, my sexuality, my needs and my dreams through the months of struggle and difficult times.

I learned so much through this time of depression. I was hurt by the comments of many priests who knew nothing of the reasons for the change from Macleod to Yarraville, but just saw me as someone wanting to get his own way. It took me a few months to get back on top of these feelings of depression and loneliness. They were hard months, and for awhile I was ready to move away from the priesthood. Emerging from this time, I had a strong feeling of urgency for change.

As I have already mentioned, I have never been a champion of celibacy as a way of life. This particular episode is one of many difficult times along the way. Most frustrating for me is the attitude of the Church towards an open discussion of celibacy as instanced by a couple of stories.

At a senate of priests meeting in our zone several years ago, one of our priests had been away to a training week to prepare priests to be available as spiritual directors in the local area. In his report, he spoke of celibacy as 'that precious jewel'. Strangely, nobody challenged this. Perhaps I was the one out of line. Anyway, I said that I wished celibacy were such a 'jewel' for me as life might then be easier. For me it had been a necessary condition to becoming a priest. I had never liked it, was still struggling with it and probably would always struggle with it. As far as I was concerned it was not a 'freely chosen gift' but a necessary burden if one wanted to be a priest.

In a discussion with a priest several years ago, the conversation led eventually to sexuality. He spoke about masturbation. In his fifteen years of priesthood, he had never spoken to anyone else about it. He always felt that he was letting down the priesthood. He had been trained to be strong, to be pure and to be alone. He had carried a sense of guilt for years.

On another occasion, I went to a priest for confession. It was at the time of a rough patch in my early years. I hesitated about approaching this priest because I thought it may upset him. But I did it. By coincidence, within a week, a young woman talked to me about a problem. She was worried because a priest had been making advances to her. My confessor of the previous week! During my visit he had sat back chiding me, reminding me of my commitment. While I wanted some understanding, I received judgment. Why couldn't he have replied 'I understand. I struggle too'?

Many years ago a friend of mine suggested that a group of priests should get together and do a questionnaire to find out what priests really thought about celibacy. My reply then, and I suppose it may have changed a bit in recent years, was that it would be difficult because the priests would only give the expected answers and not the real answers.

At a seminar for priests in Melbourne some years ago, I was asked to be a group leader. At the training day for leaders, we were shown how to tackle the question of celibacy by starting with marriage! From the lived-out marriage commitment of love, we would be able to draw parallels for ourselves in the living out of our celibacy. At the seminar I asked the group, as instructed, to go off by themselves and list five things that helped them to live out the celibate life. The answers came back and included prayer, support of priests, friends etc. However, one thing given as a help was 'broken marriages, especially of priests who have left'. This response saddened me. I had actually written down 'beautiful marriages'.

Then we had to list five things which made living the celibate life difficult. As I sat in the sun, I pondered this question and made two lists and showed them to a priest, Father Gerry Dowling, who is a professional counsellor. I felt that my first list was predictable, namely loneliness, lack of support, tiredness, too much work, non-supportive parish priest, bad living situation and the like. But I had made a second list. The first word on the list was breasts (although I used the colloquial word!), the second was testicles (again, a more colloquial word was used!), followed by some other interesting 'difficulties'. We both had a good laugh about the list and commented on how interesting it would be to discuss these in the group. After a start with the expected answers, I decided to have a go. I was encouraged by roars of laughter coming from a nearby room where Gerry Dowling was leading a group!

Of course the second list brought a bit of laughter. The point I made then—and now—is simply that because of our sexuality, celibacy ought to be difficult. Breasts (again, the colloquial!) represented female sexuality, and testicles (or whatever word!) represented our own sexuality. This sexuality is a real and good thing in our lives. As priests, we often don't own our sexuality and our natural feelings which may involve taking risks in getting close to people.

The battle for me goes on and will continue to go on. Both my working situation with a team of people and my living situation with others have developed and given me support and made it far easier for me to live and love as a priest.

Yarraville

My first year in Yarraville, 1975, can be looked back upon as an 'angry year'. I saw so many things in the Church which were 'wrong'. From my angry point of view there was hardly anything to be said in favour of the Church in Melbourne at this time. The fact that I had remained in the priesthood was due to the support and influence of some priests who helped me. Because of them I am still a priest. It is a sadness to me that some of them left the active ministry, but I can never forget what they gave me during this angry year—a belief in myself and my call to serve as a priest.

During this year Archbishop Little was probably tired of my visits to his office. Four times I approached him, and three of these visits were directly concerned with my thoughts about ministry in Yarraville. In previous years I had talked with the archbishop about the need for new forms of ministry, particularly for team ministry with lay and religious people. I'm sure there were times when I must have bored him with all my ideas, but he kept on receiving me and listening to me.

I felt strongly that there must be other ways of ministering as a priest in a parish. The present structures did not necessarily have to survive into the future. New ways of ministering must be found, and these ways must involve the laity in a shared responsibility. There must be other forms of support for priests, besides the presbytery style of living. Perhaps this could be found somewhere in team ministry, but not a team of priests. In some areas, such as Yarraville, there was a need for the Church to speak to the lives of the people and the conditions of the world in which they lived and worked. So many things occupied my mind at this time.

Early in 1976 I wrote a long letter to the archbishop outlining a proposal for me to work from a house just up the street from the presbytery. The house was available for twelve months. This would give it the opportunity to be considered an experiment. My cousin, Thelma Lacey, was ready to move with me into this project. We had worked out a way of funding the whole thing ourselves. I sent off the letter, waited an appropriate time and then rang for an appointment. Before leaving, I said to Thelma, 'Well, this is it, Thelma. If the archbishop says yes, we're on our way. If he says no, we're still on our way'. So I headed off for my interview with all my arguments for the proposal ready. After the preliminary chatter with the archbishop, I began proceedings by asking 'Well, what did you think of my letter?' To which the archbishop replied that he thought it was a beautiful letter. Well, that took me by surprise. I asked him what this meant.

The archbishop indicated that I could go ahead with the proposal and it had his full support.

I was a bit taken aback and said to him 'That's great, but what about all the arguments I've got ready to give you in reply to your objections?' We laughed and had a great yarn about the proposal, and I experienced the archbishop's support for it also. He had only two conditions for me. The first was that the parish should pay the rent and other costs, and not myself. The second was that I must ensure that I had a holiday each year. I felt these two provisions were not too hard to accept.

Moving into an 'open house' The time had come to begin. I had this house down the street for a year. I had the permission from the archbishop to make a start. My cousin Thelma was going to live at the house. The parish council had listened to the project and had given its support. So let's go!

Thelma and I had decided that one of the main features of the open house approach would be the table. People would be welcome to share a meal with us at any time. One of the great gifts of people in Yarraville is hospitality. We should be able to meet gift with gift. It's a whole new world to meet people over a meal or a cup of tea. The table was a central point in the open house approach at our new home or the 'parish centre' as it soon became known.

People started coming through the door which was kept open at most times. We were available whenever we were home. Because it was an experiment, we kept a record of everyone who came to the house in the first six months. I was going to bombard the archbishop with figures at the end of the year. After six months we came to realise that these figures meant nothing. This open house was not about numbers of people. It could only be about individuals. Each and every person who walked through the door or who rang on the telephone had to be special. Individual people, that was the key.

Those first twelve months were exciting. Both Thelma and I could see possibilities beginning to emerge. All we needed was the chance to move into this new field.

In Yarraville, I lived and worked for six years in three different houses in this 'open house' style. During those days I would often be asked, especially by priests, 'What exactly do you do?' It was difficult to explain that there was no pattern to what was happening. Should I draw a picture of a string of people coming to the house one after another, so that there is hardly time to have a decent meal? Now and again such a day would happen. But on other days maybe no-one called for the entire day. There is simply no set pattern to life once the door has been opened and you have made yourself available.

Somewhere between those two extremes is the reality. Life had become full of unexpected opportunities and joys—moments to reach out and discover Christ present in people at the time they chose.

Towards the end of 1981 I felt that it was time for me to move on and step aside from all that was happening in Yarraville. The foundations had been laid with the education of the parish council and the development of a team of people working full-time in the parish. My task had been to lay this foundation. Someone else needed to build upon it.

I suggested to some of the Personnel Board of the archdiocese that whoever was coming to Yarraville should perhaps have three months warning and be part of the planning for the following year. There would be eight people working in a parish team in 1982 with the new priest as the leader of that team. The planning for the next year would be carried out in November and December, and as leader, the new priest should be part of that planning. The immediate response was that it would be hard to find someone wanting to live in this way, so I contacted and interviewed three priests and gave their names to the personnel board. I was also told that an earlier appointment was not possible.

In November, Father Laurie Pearson was appointed to take my place at Yarraville. Laurie took part in our planning for the 1982 year. At our full day of reflection and planning led by Father Paul Hassell, I went for a walk in the garden while next year's team was planning their agenda for the coming year. It was a strange feeling to be walking in the garden at the Columban missionary house while the team of eight were inside planning without me.

I have a beautiful memory of the annual 'Thank You' night at Yarraville at the end of 1981. After thanking the people who had worked in the parish during the year, I called forward the new team for 1982. Having called them on to the stage, I then stepped down and pointed to them, and said, 'Let's give a great round of applause to next year's team'. Looking at the team for the coming year I could feel satisfied that I had laid a strong foundation for the ongoing work in Yarraville.

This left me in 'limbo' because there were no vacancies around the archdiocese for myself. The archbishop suggest that I should have a quiet time for eighteen months, until a parish became vacant. I was far from happy with that idea. Instead, I began looking at ways in which I could be effectively ministering until a parish became available. I prepared all sorts of models of work for myself. Then, because of the illness of the parish priest, Father Kevin Quinlan, the parish of West St Kilda was declared vacant. I had my ideas about where I was best suited and a place like St Kilda wasn't part of that picture. Like most people, due to the media image of the area, I thought of St Kilda as a place of drugs, crime, prostitution and street kids. Again, with the advice of priest friends, I decided that perhaps this could be the place for me and I applied for the parish.

West St Kilda

I arrived at West St Kilda as parish priest on 23 January 1982. The next day I celebrated my birthday. In retrospect, I can look back and say that it was a terrific birthday present! It took only a couple of months to have the feeling that I was at home in St Kilda. In fact, I felt that everything in my past life had been a preparation for my real ministry, which was about to begin at St Kilda.

The two-storey presbytery at West St Kilda contained seven bedrooms and at the time of my arrival was inhabited by myself and Father Michael Shadbolt. The first parish newsheet on Sunday, 31st January carried a cartoon on the front page which said 'House Full!'

I invited people to come and live at the presbytery and share our lives in St Kilda—something new was already underway. Kate Wilson arrived to work with me in the parish. Jim Finlayson and Father Denis Sheehan moved in. Father Paul Gurry came for awhile as did Father Eugene Comer from Venezuela. Then there was Kim Seiku, a young Malaysian student who came as our housekeeper for awhile. The presbytery was always a full house until we eventually moved to houses in Robe Street. At St Kilda I have always been sharing life and work with other people.

Kate and I decided that we would have plenty of time to slowly develop things in St Kilda. We would take time to listen, talk, walk and generally get the feel of the area for the first year. We began by opening the front door as a sign of welcome and hospitality to see what would happen. What happened was that people started to come in the front door and stay for awhile. We began to understand that there was much more to this area than the obvious picture presented by the media and by the popular talk about St Kilda.

We discovered an incredible world of loneliness for all sorts of reasons. As well as the obvious factors of St Kilda, namely drugs, prostitution and street kids, we came face to face with the loneliness of migrants, refugees, elderly people and others through psychiatric illness, intellectual disability, alcoholism or senility problems. This was certainly a totally different world to what we had been expecting.

Sacred Heart Mission In response to the needs, various activities began to develop in West St Kilda—an organised way to provide a meal each day for people, an 'Open House' ministry with the assistance of a good number of volunteers from the parish, care for the sick and elderly people and the development of liturgy in the church. We were somewhat 'rough and ready' during those first couple of years, but there was plenty of vitality and enjoyment as we began to build a parish community around the Eucharist.

In the first year we spent one Sunday with about eighty people from the parish just planning the future for our parish. In small groups, the parishioners were invited to express what they saw as the needs of the parish and the area and the ways in which we, as a Christian community, could respond. We have endeavoured to maintain this level of consultation with people over the years.

As the range of types of care grew, so did the size of the parish team working either part-time or full-time. The financial requirements of the various activities were growing and Government funding became available. With this growth, it became necessary to form an executive committee to be responsible for the management of this care programme. The Sacred Heart Mission was thus officially constituted in 1984.

At the beginning of 1986, the presbytery became the 'Mission House' which was now being used as the 'Open House' and as the offices for the mission team. We, the residents, moved around the corner to a house owned by the parish where we could continue to live together as the Mission continued to grow to its present size.

The journey continues

The twenty-five years of my journey as a priest is continuing to unfold. The stories and events which follow are points along that journey. There have been high and low points—times of growth and success, the times of apparent failure, the times of smiles and the times of tears, but through it all there have always been people. People have walked with me in all those moments and have shared this journey with me. My journey is about people.

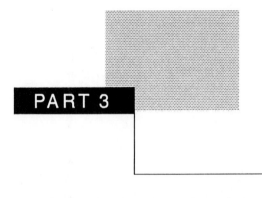

PART 3

Building a Christian community

CHAPTER 6

A Missionary Church in the City

Many of the stories in this book focus on the 'welfare' side of things. But it is necessary to point out that all this happened as part of the life of the local parish church—the local parish community. In St Kilda where there has been a remarkable growth of the Sacred Heart Mission, I always stress that it has been the people of St Kilda parish community who have taken up the challenge to become a missionary church in the local area.

It was never planned that there would be a large welfare organisation known as Sacred Heart Mission. That happened over time as the life of the parish developed and changed. 'Mission', meaning the welfare side, and 'Parish', meaning the worship or spiritual side, have grown hand in hand with each other. Both have been dependent upon each other. The Mission could not have emerged and developed without the parish base. The parish could not have developed without the Mission involvement and care for people. Together they have created an integrated model of Church in St Kilda.

There is a big wide world outside. There are people. It would be easy to stay 'inside' and not open the door to people. This reminds us what Father Quoist states in his '*Prayers of Life*'

Lord, why did you tell me to love all menmy brothers?
Lord, I was so peaceful at home, so comfortably settled.
You have forced me to open my door
        Outside men were lying in wait for me
I did not know they were so near
        As soon as I started to open my door, I saw them.

During my seminary days, I had been impressed by a visitor, Father John Whiting. He had begun a congregation of priests and brothers called the Confraternity of Christ the Priest. The aim of this new congregation was to reach the 'unchurched masses' in our communities. I suppose that I was drawn to this because I had come from the 'unchurched'. I stayed at his parish in northern Queensland on two occasions exploring whether to join the congregation. This experience helped me to fashion my own ideas.

Father Whiting and I were basically thinking in the same direction, but there were differences. His model was about a team of priests and brothers working an intensive apostolate in a parish and then handing it back to the local community. I saw the role of the lay person, in team, as essential. Father Whiting saw a direct evangelising role as essential, whereas I saw presence as the starting point and evangelisation then comes from witness.

The point is that the Church must always be thinking and moving 'out' from itself. The world beyond our congregation and our own activities needs the Church and its witness. The local parish model may have changed in recent years, but this shortcoming may still be present in many places. Is the parish community reaching out? It may not be. This could be because priests and people don't understand this challenge. However, with a large congregation, a big school and the various church organisations, it may be seen as too difficult to do any more. But there is a great mass of people who need the Church and the message of Jesus outside that congregation and those activities and services.

Yarraville and St Kilda are not large congregation parishes. In St Kilda, it is estimated that 4 per cent of people attend church, and that's the total of all the churches. We know that we are a missionary church because for every person in a pew, there are another twenty-four people not in a pew! When we think in this way, we arrive at a different set of guidelines and priorities in many aspects of church life.

Looking beyond our boundaries

What we may need on occasion are people to open the door so that we can see the people waiting for us to care for their needs. This sums up what happened when we invited people working in our local community to address the parish councillors at Yarraville. They made us see what was happening in our immediate world of Yarraville. They also challenged us to respond in some form of action. We could not sit back and do nothing—we had seen !

When Helen Wright, from the Catholic Family Welfare Bureau, spoke of the many facets of work of the bureau, she focused on one particular need, that of emergency accommodation. The bureau was desperately short of both volunteers and cash and we were challenged.

From her visit an auxiliary was formed. A group of ladies took on the job of raising money for the emergency houses, cleaning up the houses after the families moved on and helping at the bureau in various ways. This group of ladies gave a lot of help and support over many years. It came about

71

because we had someone like Helen to open the door and let us see the needs of people waiting to be met.

Frank Purcell was the organiser of the Western Region Committee for the Aging. Frank gave us facts and figures which presented the parish council with a close look at the needs of elderly people in our own area. The door was again opened. Again there were people waiting. The challenge— what can we do? From this evening some ladies attended a training course in home care of sick or elderly people. Others attended a seminar on the increasing needs of elderly people in the western suburbs.

The real fruit appeared much later with the starting of our Friendship Club. The parish provided the place and the people to be involved. The hospital provided the people to be cared for—elderly people needing help after being in the hospital. This was not a parish group for parish people. It was run in the parish and by the parish, but it was involvement in the wider community.

Pat Connolly, a nursing sister at the local baby health centre, told us of her work with mothers in stress and the problems facing young mothers in our area. She highlighted the needs of migrant women through ignorance or through language barriers. Her prayerful Christian approach to her work was in itself an inspiration, but the examples she gave were an eye-opener to us.

As a result, the contact between our own playgroup and the health centres increased, with many young mothers being sent to the playgroup from the health centres. These sorts of relationships of the Church with the wider community are necessary.

Frank Plata, a financial counsellor, gave example after example of people in trouble because of finance and the extent to which this damaged their whole life. The facts and figures really left no option but to accept the challenge. In addition to an immediate financial donation towards the work of the committee employing the financial counsellor, the parish council became involved in the development of this service.

Gift of hospitality

When I approached the archbishop about moving from the presbytery in Yarraville, one of the reasons was 'to meet the people at the level of their gift'. I use the word 'gift' often because it speaks about people and what they have to offer of themselves. A gift is freely given and that was certainly the case with hospitality in the parish of Yarraville.

People in Yarraville are friendly. They talk to each other on the street. Many have lived there all their lives. People know their neighbours. Not all parishes or suburbs are like this.

The challenge in moving to the house as a parish centre was to get across to the people a message of hospitality. Just as I had been made so welcome in their homes and found myself at kitchen tables having a cup of tea, I wanted the parish centre to be the same. Just as I was invited for a meal, I wanted to do the same. Just as I was asked to attend a celebration in someone's home, I wanted to ask people to our celebrations. I wanted the parish centre to be a place of openness, warmth, friendliness and hospitality.

To encourage people to come to the house, we arranged various activities such as an Italian class for women, flower making, cards. 'Hospitality nights' were also arranged. Five couples took turns to act as hosts and their job was to invite people to come along to an evening at the parish centre. They visited the people at home and on the night welcomed people to the centre and introduced them to each other. People met each other and enjoyed each other's company. In particular, non-Catholic husbands and wives received a welcome from a church which they had perhaps never felt before. People who were not involved in any way with the activities of the Church, and perhaps not even attending Mass, were given a welcome. On these nights, a lot of barriers were broken down and angry points were diffused.

The hospitality nights in Glenhuntly, Yarraville and now St Kilda, have been light-hearted and enjoyable. We set out to have people meet each other and for the priest and team to be part of this, and it certainly happened. As a variation, we have had hospitality barbecues or dinners, again with the same arrangements. The people came and brought themselves, while the parish did the rest. It was not to be 'Bring a plate'. People have brought enough plates to church functions, so on these days people are guests of the church. Come along and sample our hospitality. That's the message.

Saint Paul told us Christians to 'extend hospitality to strangers' (Romans 12:13). Hospitality is a very special gift which we all have to offer. Often the simple things of life give the meaning to life.

Sharing the meal table

Having an open table is a great asset even if at times a little demanding. The cup of tea was always on when people came to the parish centre at Yarraville. This can be a very positive start to meeting a person. It's a big difference to being ushered into a parlour or an office. The person is able to settle down and relax a bit. If a person is someone 'away' from the Church for a long time or has problems to talk about, what better way to begin.

Inviting people for a meal, particularly for Sunday dinner, gives an opportunity to meet people at a new level of friendship. I always find it good to meet people and to be with people, so I enjoy having people for dinner. The meal table has been a special place and an essential place in my own life.

At Yarraville, Thelma was always there for the welcome and the cuppa. It's that welcoming presence which holds the key to this approach. It was the same approach which Kate and I used on our arrival at St Kilda. So much happened over a cuppa and a chat at the kitchen table in those early days. The meals around our little kitchen table gave us the start to so much that was to follow.

Over the years at both Yarraville and St Kilda, there have been some wonderful gatherings which have brought people together, especially for celebrations. There has been the wedding reception around our table, the cuppa after the funeral, the special birthday, but above all, there has been life and enjoyment around the table.

Since moving from the big presbytery to our house around the corner, we have maintained the need to have a table that is always open to visitors. This has enabled us to share the life of people around us.

Football

I've always enjoyed a game of football, as long as I can remember. And I enjoyed it for a long time, playing my last game when I was forty-six years old! After school, it was the YCW team at Ascot Vale. During seminary it was among ourselves at the college or against any teams willing to risk life and limb playing against the student priests. I played with various teams as a priest—North Old Boys (the college where I had been some fifteen years earlier), YCW teams at Sandringham and Glenhuntly, and finally at Footscray Technical College Old Boys while at Yarraville.

At Sandringham, a new team was formed which I coached. I enjoyed two years with these fellows. I remember well the first game with this newly formed club and the great excitement. We may not have won the premiership, but we managed to forge some good friendships in those couple of years with this new club. In my next parish, Glenhuntly, the YCW team gave me a good welcome. I had three years with them which gave me the opportunity to meet many people and form lasting friendships. On to Yarraville and, after a few months, I was invited by a couple of young men from the parish to come along for a run with their football team, Footscray Tech Old Boys. But at thirty-six my playing days were over. However, my 'addiction' took over again, and I began a nine-year association with the club. During this time I was involved as a player, assistant coach, and committee member. I spent much time with this club and felt that this time was well spent. I was held in high respect as a priest among the players and their families and had plenty of fun times.

Sadly, I broke my connections with the club. Like many other sporting clubs at that time, the committee turned to 'stripper nights' to raise money. When I heard the details of one of these nights I felt that I would have to resign. I felt compromised as a priest and as a Christian. Because I enjoyed football and the company of the players, it was a hard decision. I don't regret my action, but I did miss the action of the game and the club. Over the years, I have kept in touch with some of these people and still have a 'soft spot' for the club.

Football has been good to me. The sport has provided me with the opportunity for friendships and enjoyment over many years and been a point of contact with so many people in the broader community. Many joys have come my way from the relationships formed through football, and there has been sadness shared with families.

AIDS

Responding to opportunities has taken me into aspects of life which I have not experienced before. Drugs and prostitution had not been part of my life before coming to St Kilda. Nor had homosexuality or the 'gay scene' been a significant part in my ministry as a priest. Recent years have changed this.

I became interested and involved in the HIV-AIDS question several years ago. Plenty of reading and attendance at seminars preceded my first meetings with people who had contracted this illness. I have learned about homosexuality and the struggle for acceptance by families and society. I have shared the isolation and rejection encountered through this illness. I have heard the prejudice and ignorance expressed by people within our church. I have struggled with my own feelings on occasion. And on the journey with people, both the ill and the carers, I have learned so much about life and love.

Ministering in this area of life has often taken me to places where the Church is not usually present. Gay men often do not feel 'at home' in our church pews, and drug-using young people are not usually part of our congregation. These are the main risk behaviour areas. How easy it is to judge people. Involvement in this area of illness and care takes you behind the labels to the person suffering.

'Peter' died of AIDS. He lived on my street. I knocked on his door, not knowing his name or what sort of welcome to expect. He was a Catholic, but he quickly warned me not to expect a last-minute confession! This man was at peace with himself and his God. He was more concerned for his family and friends. Over the weeks, we established a friendship and respect for each other. When Peter died, his body laid at home until the day of the funeral, and I led the procession of the coffin from the house to the church. A public procession! People like Peter can teach us to 'stand tall' when our hearts are at peace with ourselves, our family and friends, and our God.

'Margaret' was a beautiful young woman who, by chance, contracted AIDS. She and her family showed great love and support for each other through a difficult struggle. What a privilege to enter into the life of this lovely young woman. Margaret showed courage and patience as the disease racked her young body. She was not afraid to tell people that she had AIDS. Then people had to decide for themselves to love her and walk with her. It was a journey of love which culminated in the sadness of her death. A privileged learning experience for our parish was the talk given at Mass by her mother as part of World AIDS Day.

My experiences over several years helped establish an Archdiocesan AIDS Committee. One of the first undertakings was the education of priests towards a better knowledge and understanding of the illness. This has been rewarding. As with so many facets of life, ignorance breeds fear. Knowledge and experience opens us to the opportunity for loving.

Taking the Church to the workplace

In Glenhuntly, I was invited to become an industrial chaplain. This meant attending a factory or other workplace on a regular basis, officially serving as chaplain to all the workers. It was an ecumenical undertaking. I declined the offer because there were no factories in the area and I would be travelling a fair distance from my own area to be a chaplain. I appreciated the concept as it gave the opportunity to reach out into the broader community, taking the Church to the working place of people, meeting them where they were in their world.

When I was appointed to Yarraville, I felt that this was a different situation. Now I was living and working in the midst of a factory area, and the majority of men and women worked in factories. I applied for a chaplaincy and was appointed to the I.C.I. chemical factory and also to the Albright & Wilson factory. I received my special jacket and 'hard hat' which identified me as the chaplain to all the workers. I was following other men from other Christian traditions, so I had a welcome immediately.

My first impression of factory life was a shock. As I said at the time to friends, 'I had forgotten what factory life could be like'. I had seen and been part of factories before, but this was like a first experience. A chemical factory meant dust and smell, often to an overpowering degree. How those men worked there on some days was beyond me. The first few weeks were spent getting to know the workers slowly. Then my own 'work' began. Stopping for a chat, having a cuppa here, listening to a small worry there, just walking and stopping wherever, moving around the factory complexes. My hours at the factory increased because the walk took longer as I came to know the people. In both places, I had the opportunity to be with and assist people in a variety of ways. It was not always to fulfil a spiritual need, but I always felt that the Church was reaching people where they were working. This was the important fact.

During this time as industrial chaplain, I received an invitation to attend the Modern Maid factory in Footscray. The factory had been threatened with closure, but the workers joined together to buy the business. It was a significant effort in the business world. The new management of the factory had an official opening day. As part of this, I was invited to speak and give a blessing to the factory and the workers. Sadly, some years later, the factory eventually closed down. But the factory's closing does not detract from the importance of the opening day blessing. The Church, through the presence of an industrial chaplain, was present to the workers in an important event.

Getting involved

In St Kilda, parishioners were the first 'workers'. They helped to prepare meals, do the shopping and mind the house. There were always people to give a hand. That same spirit of people getting involved continued, not only with the hall meal and the open house, but in the clinic and the women's ministry, Op Shop and Mass for the elderly people. Whatever the call to help, people responded. The parishioners in St Kilda have plenty of opportunities to become involved. Time and again a variety of invitations are extended which seek help in all sorts of ways.

Restoration of a church building

The restoration of the beautiful old church of the Sacred Heart was completed in April 1991. Built in 1884 at the height of St Kilda's pre-eminence among the suburbs of Melbourne, it had fallen into decay. The ceiling was punctured with holes, the rain was causing extreme damage and the walls were badly cracked. It was a sad and sorry state for one of the old beautiful churches of the city. When I arrived in 1982, there was no possible way in which the parish community could accept the task of renovation. The financial resources were not present.

In 1987 we celebrated the parish's centenary and began an appeal for the restoration. Towards the end of 1988, a special meeting of parishioners was held in the church, and the committee presented two possible plans for the church restoration one costing $150 000 and the other costing $180 000. A vote was taken and it was unanimous that we should proceed with the more expensive option. As with any restoration task, the cost was far greater than expected and eventually reached $450,000. As the parish community continued to grow in strength, so did the financial response. It is hoped that this commitment will be met in as little as five years.

Speaking at the dedication mass to mark the completion of this enormous undertaking for our parish, I suggested a bit of theology. If we, the parish, had undertaken to restore the old building without caring for the people of the area, this would have been a 'mortal sin'. If we had fed people and done great things in the welfare area while we let the beautiful old church fall further into decay, this also could have been seen as a 'mortal sin'. However, to do both may be a means of 'grace' for us. In other words, to be an integrated or complete people of God in St Kilda, both responses were equally important.

Over the years, the attendance at the Sunday Masses has grown, and this is encouraging. But it's not just numbers. What is more encouraging is the number of people who have found a welcome in our congregation. On any Sunday, the congregation includes so many people who are broken through various addictions, feeling on the outer of the Church because of marriage situations, searching for meaning to their lives, trying to rediscover the Church they had left behind many years before. The congregation itself, in its make-up, is a source of great consolation and affirmation for the work of the Mission.

I've said nothing about the 'normal' activities of our parish. I feel that the spirit engendered through the work of the Mission touches the ministry of the Church through the school, social life, playgroup and other aspects of parish life. It's all one.

No need for a blueprint

So what about the future? Perhaps the best way of understanding the challenge of the future is to learn from our experience in the past. In Yarraville, when I moved into the house up the street, and in St Kilda, when we opened the front door, we did not have a plan which stated concrete objectives for the next one, two or five years. What I had with Thelma in Yarraville and what I had with Kate in St Kilda, was an attitude of responding to needs as they appeared. We did not go out looking for problems, but we waited to see what the world was asking of us.

Our St Kilda experience spells out this attitude. What began as a simple sharing of our kitchen table with a few people in 1982 became a daily meal in our parish hall for 100 people in 1983. By 1991, over 300 people were coming to the hall each day in a highly organised daily meal program. It simply grew as we responded to the needs of people. When two chiropractors offered their professional services in 1989, we did not envisage that in 1992 there would be a separate clinic with a coordinator, a team of volunteers and fifteen professional people giving their services. The opportunity was presented, and we responded because we could help people. We dabbled in our care of people in the special accommodation houses of the area for some years before deciding that we should be managing a place ourselves. Several failed efforts from 1987 led us to rent a property in 1989. Now the Government has funded the Mission for the purchase of that property. The Mission moved into this area after years of soul-searching about the needs of these extremely poor people of St Kilda.

A similar approach can be seen in the ministry to women, the housing program, the art and recreation activities. There was always the need of the people challenging us or the offer to care extended to us. My own approach to the future is simple. I believe that the future will unveil itself if we live the present very fully. In the present we have to be able to see the opportunities, the challenges, the call and the people, and grasp all of these in our hands and in our hearts.

The world is there and the church is in its midst. It's about being a missionary church in the city. That's the bottom line surely. The people are there and their lives make the life of the church. The opportunities are there, if we are open to see and hear and respond to the situation at hand.

CHAPTER 7

Life Shared with Others

Open house in Yarraville

Shortly after I was ordained in 1968, I was invited by a couple of priests, Val Noone and Garry McLoughlin, to be part of a team ministry which they were hoping to set up. I remember a meeting at Val's parents' home in Bentleigh when lots of ideas were being tossed around about models of parish and priestly life.

I would have liked to be part of their dreams at that time, but I felt that I had better wait for awhile since I was just ordained and still in the Seminary. They sowed seeds in my life. In my early years as a priest, I had a vision of a team of priests and the notion of team ministry never left me. I concocted various ideas about team ministry, most of which never got outside of my mind. However, at one point in time, I formulated a definite plan for an experimental team of priests and religious persons for a particular part of an inner-city parish. It was this plan which awakened me to the fact that team is about priest and lay people working together in mission.

In 1976, Thelma and I had been given the go ahead to put my plan into practice at the house at Yarraville, there was still planning involved and questions to be answered. Where do I begin? How do I inform the people of the parish? By moving into a local house I hoped that people would find it a little easier to approach the priest. By being able to extend hospitality in an atmosphere of openness and availability, we could give a different type of witness to people.

The parish council were the first people in the parish to discuss the new project. The councillors gave me their support and encouragement. The venture certainly demanded considerable trust in me personally, and I have always appreciated this trust and support. Once the parish council was informed, it was then necessary to inform the people. This was done through the newsletter and through a sermon at all the Masses. Some fascinating experiences occurred in those first months.

Immediately after that first Mass at which I spoke about the new parish centre, a lady approached me. She asked for an appointment for the following Tuesday evening. When she arrived at the new centre, she told me that for some months she had been trying to come to the presbytery to see me. On a couple of occasions she had actually come to the presbytery, but she had gone away without ringing the doorbell. When she heard me speak of the centre, she felt this was what she had been waiting for. She could now approach me more easily. Wow! What a great start to our new venture—my first appointment telling me this. Such a start did wonders for our optimism!

A lady rang from the railway station at Yarraville. She was speaking of suicide. After a long talk on the phone, she came to the parish centre. She was not a Catholic and not from the parish. Let's call her 'Joan' because that's how she

introduced herself. She didn't give me her real name. She
came back a couple more times and I have not seen her since.
Meeting with anonymous people and being given the
opportunity to help them, even in a small way or for a certain
time, is a very special grace for us.

And then there was 'Betty'. Again, anonymous. I don't
know where she came from or who referred her to me. She
came and that's what mattered. Betty was experiencing
certain problems with her marriage. After several meetings
with me I am sure she thought I knew who she was. We had
become good friends. Then she stopped coming. Three years
later she appeared again to say thanks for my advice. It's not
important here whether my advice was good, but simply that
she came back after three years. By the way I still don't know
where she lives or her real name!

We needed to encourage people in the beginning so a few
activities were started in the first weeks. Thelma moved into
action quickly. Three afternoons at the centre ladies came to
learn Italian, make artificial flowers or play cards. These
activities brought small groups of women together at the
parish centre and helped establish the concept of an open
house. Good and lasting friendships developed through these
early activities.

The youth meetings also moved to the parish centre.
Because the centre was also Thelma's home, these meetings
of young people took on a different style. A very relaxed
atmosphere developed as they began to feel 'at home'. A
most interesting thing happened in those early days. A group
of 'toughies' joined the YCW group and started attending the
weekly meetings which were held at 8 p.m. However, this
group began arriving at 7 p.m. They would sit and watch
television with Thelma until the meeting began. I guess the

thing they were looking for was a family and in some way Thelma was providing that experience for them.

The main thing was that people started coming through the door. Because we had no blueprint when we began, it was a matter of learning as we moved along. One of the first things we discovered was the number of lonely people waiting to be welcomed. Many of the people who became regular visitors at the centre were lonely people. All that was needed from Thelma and myself was a warm welcome, an open door and time to listen and be with people. I feel that many people who came to identify with the centre through their regular calls helped me so much; I had to be ready to stop, be with and listen to people. Time was the gift I could offer to people who came to the centre. There are so many people in our world just waiting outside the door, needing to be welcomed into our lives.

Thelma—The key to a welcome

In 1974 Thelma came to join me at the Glenhuntly presbytery as housekeeper. She was at a loose end, separated from her husband after many years of marriage, with a grown-up family and very alone. Life had little meaning for Thelma at this point in her life. She had recently returned from Brisbane, was in a bit of a 'down' period of her life and did not feel like meeting people, particularly her relatives. So she stayed in her flat drinking cups of tea by the score and popping pills to calm her nerves. To put it very simply, Thelma was a mess.

When I went to Yarraville, there wasn't a live-in housekeeper, but very soon Thelma came to join the parish priest, Father Fasciale, and myself. When we moved to the parish centre in Yarraville in 1976, the role of housekeeper disappeared. The centre was to be her home for the next four years. Her role was basically hospitality. However, a necessary asset was a sympathetic ear. For many people in Yarraville, the centre became Thelma's place. Many people came just to see Thelma.

There was always a warm welcome at the centre because Thelma was there. People could stop, talk and have a cup of tea. They could simply hang around for awhile. They could cry. They could do whatever they felt like because Thelma was there. After all, this was Thelma's place.

As far as I was concerned, I could do all those same things too. I could get a warm welcome, stop, talk, have a cup of tea or even cry (yes, that too!) because Thelma was there. During those years together my life changed a great deal. My way of working changed too. Thelma helped me to do this.

Many people quickly became regulars at the parish centre, dropping in for a cup of tea and a chat. I can vividly remember one woman, Pat, calling at the centre. She had been in a bit of trouble earlier on with her family. After talking with her waiting for her to 'open up', I asked her if she would like a cup of tea. Only then I realised that she had no problems. She had just popped in to say hello. It's so easy to become 'problem seekers'.

One of Thelma's important tasks was to keep me healthy. I must admit to being somewhat spoiled during this time. There was always a meal ready for me whatever time I arrived home. Because we worked closely together, Thelma came to know me and could anticipate my needs. She knew how to tempt me with food and would prepare something a little special to make me stop for awhile. This was good for me.

I remember those nights when someone would leave the centre in the early hours of the morning. Thelma would emerge from her room and put the kettle on for a cup of tea. This bit of company and relaxation over a cup of tea was a great help to me.

The night Thelma was received into the Church was a joyous occasion. It was a revelation for many people that Thelma was not a Catholic and had been working for the church. The news spread. Before a crowded Saturday night congregation, with great celebration, Thelma took a step that was to bring her a new peace from a faith she shared with so many. Afterwards every room of the centre and the outside area was filled with happy people. These were the people who had come to love Thelma so much. They were now rejoicing with her.

However, the greatest testimony to the important role that belonged to Thelma was her farewell in 1979. Most people would have one farewell. Thelma had a week of them. Each group in the parish seemed to be having celebrations at that time, and Thelma always featured in the celebration—the youth surprised her, the elderly surprised her, the parish welfare committee surprised her, the parish council surprised her and many individual people came to say their own farewells.

No wonder that I had difficulty getting through a thank-you speech at the parish council night and making a presentation to Thelma. So much had been achieved at the centre in the years of Thelma's service. So much was due to her contribution. Thelma can teach us a lesson about ministry in the Church. It's a lesson about gifts.

Thelma's great gift was herself. Her life and situation gave her a way to touch the lives of people with her own special gift. It was a gift that needed to be given the chance to flourish. From being sad, alone, depressed and with little purpose in life, Thelma had become vital, caring and loving. Her life was full of people to touch with that gift of herself.

A tribute to Thelma is a challenge to recognise in all people the gift which they are, and to give the opportunity and

the space for that gift to grow. To speak of ministry may well
be a case of speaking about gifts.

First pastoral workers

It was decided in 1977 that we needed lay people to work in
Yarraville and that the immediate areas of concern were
youth, young women and the elderly people. It wasn't
financially possible and probably not wise pastorally anyway,
to launch into a big programme, but we could at least make a
start.

Colleen Charles was the first pastoral worker. Colleen
began in 1977. Her role was to conduct the playgroup for
young women and their children and also to carry out
visitation and contact work within this group. This was a new
step and there were worries about how Colleen would be
accepted within the parish. Colleen and the subsequent lay
pastoral workers were well received and appreciated by the
people they visited and cared for.

Colleen was married with three children, but had returned
to the parish about eighteen months earlier after leaving her
husband. At that time she had five-year-old twins and a babe
a few months old. With a marriage at an end, it would have
been easy for Colleen to be seen as another 'case' of a solo
parent raising a family. However, Colleen had begun to show
her qualities of leadership and her capacity to understand the
situations of other women through her own struggle. Like
Thelma, much of her gift came from her own life situation of
suffering and heartache decisions.

Being on a pension, Colleen was able to earn a limited
amount for her two days' work visiting people in the parish.
Colleen was employed on a part-time basis for nine years.
This sort of work is not about hours, but about people. It
involves a commitment to serve people whenever and
wherever the need arises.

Just a few months later the second person, Joan Perussich, was approached. Joan had nursed her husband Spencer through cancer and he had died at home in 1975. It was during this time that the gifts of Joan had become obvious to me—gentleness, patience, kindness and understanding.

At this time Joan was forty-seven, too young for the widow's pension. She was expected to find a job after twenty-seven years as mother and housewife and in a time of high unemployment. Joan, like both Thelma and Colleen, brought her special ministry in the parish, her gifts stemming from personal suffering and difficulty.

Joan was employed by the parish on the same basis as Colleen. A couple of days each week visiting people, but in this case Joan would be concentrating her attention on the elderly and lone people in the parish.

At this point, what is so special about Colleen and Joan? After all, there are many people who have carried out just this type of work for many years without being on the payroll. The parish council had discussed this matter at great length, and some of the main reasons put forward at that time are worth sharing.

Employing two people, as distinct from volunteers, would demand a greater commitment from the parish and from the council, both financially and in support and encouragement. A new relationship would be established between the priests and these pastoral workers because they would be co-workers. As priests have so often found, it is hard to keep asking people to do jobs. In this case, Colleen and Joan could be asked to take on tasks because they were employed—it's their job. Finally, a new relationship would be established between the lay workers and the parishioners. They would have to be seen as not merely helping the priests, but carrying out an important task in our parish community. This was considered to be an important question and something of a concern.

However, the parish was very understanding and accepting of the ministry of lay people.

At the end of 1977, during which year both Colleen and Joan had settled into their new role in Yarraville, the parish council made another decision. It was decided to employ someone to work with the youth of the parish. Terry and Jenny Chessels were a young married couple with a brand new baby, Michael. Jenny had a background of YCW experience and had spent four years as a lay missionary in New Guinea. Her work in the missions had been the establishment of groups for native women in the villages and also the training of village women as leaders of these groups. On her return to Melbourne, Jenny was looking for some way of continuing her mission experience and Church involvement. For eighteen months she worked as a youth worker in the parish of Hawthorn until her marriage and the birth of her child.

Jenny was looking towards parish involvement again, in a way that would involve her husband also. The parish provided a house for the Chessels which would be their home, but also a centre for the young people as a meeting place and point of reference.

Given the obvious limitations of a young baby, Jenny began working with the youth committees and visiting the families of young people. Her husband, Terry, was also involved in this apostolate, again within the limitations of his own work as an ambulance driver. What was good news for Terry and Jenny was to make their task impossible; during this year of 1978 they had a second child, Christopher.

Things did not work out as planned with Terry and Jenny for the obvious reasons, but their contribution was important in this year. They helped to pave the way for lay people to minister in the Church. A couple of years before, Jenny had said to me, in a time of anger at the attitude of the Church towards lay people, 'Do I have to be a nun to get a job in the Church of Melbourne?' In a relatively short time the climate changed and the role of lay people in the Church as ministers was being thought about and developed in some places.

Although things didn't work out for Terry and Jenny, they still continued to live on in Yarraville for quite awhile because they had made close friends in the parish. More important was the fact that the need for someone to continue their work was never questioned. The need was there, and we were going to answer the need.

Colleen, Joan, Terry and Jenny had burst open the concept of a 'priest church' and made the way clear to move towards the development of a wider parish team in the future.

Dominic—A living presence

To write about the life of the people means a special mention of one of the initiatives undertaken at Yarraville. That was the establishment of a house called 'Dominic'. It is the name given by Sister Bernadette Murphy, a Dominican Sister, to the house where she lives in one corner of the parish of Yarraville. This concept, undertaken as an experiment, was based on the value of presence. In other words merely by being present or 'being with' the people is a step in the process of evangelisation. Perhaps this venture can be best explained in the words of Pope Paul VI in his statement called 'The Evangelisation of Peoples'. In this challenging document the Pope says:

> Take a handful of Christians, who, in the midst of their own community, show their capacity for understanding and acceptance, their sharing of life and destiny with other people, their solidarity with the efforts of all for whatever is noble and good. Through wordless witness they stir up questionshere we have an initial act of evangelism.

The key word then in this 'Dominic' venture had to be 'presence', and in this particular situation the presence of a religious person in a small area of the parish. Sister Bernadette was asked to write in a special edition of our parish newsletter, at a time when we were beginning open days at 'Dominic'. Her words at this time are worth sharing now after ten years of presence in the area.

> Saint Dominic was a man who read the signs of the times and interpreted them in the light of the Gospel. Hence his aim was to seek out and preach authentically God's word for that day. I would see one of the signs of our times to be the force with which people are crying out for a new society. People today are seeking a togetherness, whereby a person feels acknowledged for what he or she is, rather than what he or she has done. If the Church can become a dynamo of love, concern and justice within the community of mankind, then the world can be changed. Within the framework of our global village, our little corner of one parish seems very small, butif we can set up a network of such cells, imagine what might happen. With confident hope already strengthened by the welcome that I have received, that this concept will become a reality, 'Dominic' has begun.

Again, there was no blueprint for action. Only time could tell the best way to be effective in this apostolate of presence in a smaller area of the parish. The ways outlined to the parishioners were Eucharist, prayer, hospitality, celebrations and visitation. These were to be the 'meeting points' for the Church and people through Sister Bernadette and 'Dominic'.

Ten years on, can we assess the results? An immediate response would be that the venture has been successful. But if you were to ask against what criterion, then it is difficult to answer. The success does not, and cannot, lie in numbers of people who come to Mass at the house, the numbers of people who frequently call in or the numbers of people visited. The answer lies in the development of a spirit of care and concern, and awareness of each other in the people of the area. This happened, but it is that intangible quality which cannot easily be measured.

In the beginning there was the weekly celebration of the Eucharist which soon developed into a community celebration. The intimacy of ten, twelve, fifteen people who were all neighbours gathering regularly to share in the Eucharist was an experience to be fully appreciated only through participation. That people came to know each other, after having only a 'head nodding' acquaintance for so many years, was a slow but sure step towards building a community of love and care.

At the end of the first year of the life of 'Dominic', Sister Bernadette presented a report to the parish council which was more a reflection than numbers of 'things' achieved. Before 'Dominic', our knowledge of the area was limited to a few names in the census, often without knowing any more than their names. Now the number of people known, and not only by names, had grown, and these people in turn came to know each other also. There were delightful examples of growth in care and in understanding of the mission of the Church.

There were 'teething problems' with 'Dominic' as with any new venture, but after a time these problems were settled. For Sister Bernadette there was the obvious separation from her community life and from the main parish centre. At times she experienced a feeling of not only separation but isolation from the mainstream of parish life and activity. At these times she needed a strong faith in the vision as outlined when the venture first began. I suppose Sister Bernadette must often have wondered whether it was all worthwhile, but now I feel confident we can see 'Dominic' as a worthwhile and significant venture in building a community in a smaller area.

The original idea about a community of people living at 'Dominic' changed as time progressed. Jan Stumbles, a tertiary student lived at 'Dominic' for a while in the early days of settling in at this new venture. Then, for more than a year, Sister Bernadette was alone with visitors staying for different periods of time. The front bedroom became a lounge, the lounge became a prayer room, and the laundry out the back became a guest room! In 1981 Pat Hecker, a friend of Sister Bernadette from Tasmania, was a welcome visitor for a couple of months and then moved in with Sister Bernadette. 'Dominic' has been their home ever since. Yes, there have been changes as time has rolled along. For Sister Bernadette it was certainly a dramatic change in lifestyle. Sister Bernadette's story, written some years ago, captures the spirit of what 'Dominic' was and still is about.

Sister Bernadette's Story

Having arrived at my destination in Yarraville, I was introduced to Sister Emilien, the superior of the St Joseph's Convent. To her I am extremely grateful for had it not been for her gracious hospitality, I can say without doubt, that 'Dominic' would never have eventuated. I lived with the Sisters of St Joseph for about twelve months, there being no Dominican Convent on this side of the city. This enabled me to find my bearings in my new parish, for it was a part of Melbourne with which I was unfamiliar.

It was not long before we realised that in this vast sprawling parish, so many people were 'untouched' by the Church. This was understandably so for much of the Church involvement had to be concentrated in a network of buildings which had built up over the years. It was also obvious that 'out there' various pockets of the parish were demanding a more concrete point of contact.

We knew that when the appropriate time dawned, something would present itself. And it did. A house was advertised in the local paper as being 'To Let', something of a rarity in the area as most houses were for private sale or auction. However, far more significant was the fact that this house was in the very centre of one pocket of the parish about which Father Smith had often 'dreamed dreams'. Without delay, various telephone calls were made and the house was ours, so that in January 1980 'Dominic' became a reality.

Each week we celebrated the Eucharist which was followed by a cup of tea, lunch or even on one occasion, a barbecue, I recall the remarks expressing gratitude for the opportunity to share the Eucharist during the week. For most of the people weekday Mass was impossible because we are so far from the church. One of my neighbours had just begun a course on pottery when I arrived. We soon boasted of having our own chalice and paten. These were the first articles she made after she had mastered a few of the pottery skills. After two years there was growth in appreciation and understanding of the Eucharist, both in daily personal life and in a community of people. The level of intimacy attained in these weekly celebrations was a lovely experience.

The development of community is certainly a slow process. We will always have a long way to go. I believe that many people became more aware of each other during those early years of 'Dominic'. Among the people in the area there were some who had been hurt by the Church in various ways over the years. We must first of all recognise this. We need to provide a climate whereby such people can talk through their experiences. In this way many of these hurts, whether real or imagined, can be healed.

There are so many identities who come to mind as I recall those early days and it would be unfair to single out people. So many supported me in different ways by doing things for me or just by being so welcoming and hospitable. 'Dominic' is really about the people of the area. People coming to know and love each other. I believe that 'Dominic' has helped this to happen.

'Dominic' is but one of many small pockets in the Yarraville parish, but it gave us the incentive to move out to the people. The effects may be hard to assess and record, and of course to share. But the vision is there, which is to move the Church out to the corners of the parish where people assume some responsibility for each other.

Religious sisters in the parish

In recent years a whole new dimension to the apostolate and presence of religious sisters in the parish scene has opened up. Today the opportunities for religious sisters are there for the taking. The role of retired religious sisters is easily fitted into parish life. Back in 1976 it was a big step for two older sisters, Sister Veronica and Sister Philomena, to work with me in the parish.

The need for visitation was great with a high number of elderly and sick people often confined to their homes, but it needed to be a special sort of visitation. Sister Veronica had a fair amount of free time, so I was able to set out on a pattern of visiting which was to bring us very close to the people and share in many joys and sorrows. Because many of the people were being brought to a regular Mass for sick people every fortnight, the demand of the regular Communion round was gone. More time could be spent with very sick people.

In those early days we managed to spend many hours visiting. As time went on however, we found that sometimes we would make only one call. It may have been a special occasion for the person. Perhaps he or she was very sick or lonely on this day. We had by now thrown away any sort of programme and did not attempt to visit so many people every so often. Over the years, Sister Veronica built up a long list of many dear friends with whom she endeavoured to keep in contact. This apostolate of loving care grew through the years and through involvement.

Sister Veronica and I still reminisce over many experiences through this time. There was a lot of fun. There were long days or weeks of waiting with people who were dying. There were tears as we mourned with people. We realised that by our visiting we often opened ourselves to being hurt by the loss of friends

> One such person was a young woman named Colleen England. Colleen was in her thirties and died of multiple sclerosis in a private hospital in Hawthorn. The priests in the parish cared for Colleen during her last weeks of life in this hospital. However, on the Saturday morning when Colleen died, I was with the family for a long time praying with them at the bedside. It was one of the most peaceful and moving deaths I have witnessed, as somewhere during the fourth decade of the rosary, Colleen stopped breathing. Her elderly mother was holding her hand and leading the rosary. I told the family that Colleen had died, and we continued to pray the rosary peacefully with tears of joy? sadness?

Moments of becoming intimately part of a family don't just happen. For years Sister Veronica and I had been visiting Colleen and her family at her home and in various hospitals, being part of the special birthday celebrations, teasing her and joking with her. We were always trying to bring joy and laughter into her life of sickness and handicap. There had been the many times when Colleen would be depressed and asking why this would happen to her, but overall her serenity and joy came through. Because we were free to spend time without any hurry with Colleen and her family, we could enter into a privileged place in her life and death.

When Nance Barnett, who had been dying for some time with cancer, took a serious turn which would immediately precede her death, word was received just as we were about to begin our Christmas party with our elderly parishioners. I went to see Nance, but took with me both Sister Veronica and Joan Perussich our parish worker. We had all been involved in constant care of Nance for a long time. It was a case of a 'team anointing' with Nance and a most peaceful occasion for all of us as we said goodbye to Nance at home before she went to the hospital. All three of us were upset as we said our goodbye for we had become close through Nance's involvement as a driver for the Mass for the elderly people and through our regular visitation and care in her sickness.

We appreciated the role of a religious sister with families. It was a role that could be developed through care and love. Sister Veronica was not young. She had her own share of sickness which included three major operations in 1978. Yet she had a new freedom to move among these people who became her close friends, reliving moments with them, sharing their joys and worries and just being with them.

Every so often Sister Veronica would be called upon to give a report on her work as part of the parish team. Invariably her report would be something in the vein of 'I've just been visiting and I've really nothing to report'. Such a statement could never have been further from the truth.

Looking for new ways to minister In 1978 Sister Maureen Beha joined the parish team. Maureen was a nurse and was released to Yarraville as an experiment to see how effectively a nursing religious sister could be involved at a parish and community level. Maureen worked in the parish for four months and was replaced in 1979 by Sister Mary Rogers who also worked for about four months. The nursing experiment opened up a new approach to the visiting and care of the sick people. Sister Maureen was able to work in conjunction with the District Nursing Service.

Depending on the locality and the need, such involvement with local community services can be an important apostolate. In Yarraville, the nursing service could not give the care or time needed because of extremely heavy work loads. The nursing talents of both these sisters were appreciated. They were involved in the wider community of Yarraville and brought quite a few non-Catholic people within the scope of our parish care. Both Sister Maureen and Sister Mary made their own special contribution in the parish.

Maureen had been accustomed to working in an infirmary where order of time was an important factor. In the parish, she had to learn that she did not have to be doing something all the time to be effective, but that sometimes it was necessary to simply be with people. What a lovely compliment it was that old Bob and Alice Slevison could say that they looked upon Maureen as a daughter who cared for them in their sickness. The warmth of a loving presence with people is surely most appreciated with sick and elderly people. Mary, not qualified to work as complement to the district nurse, brought great kindness and gentleness to her caring work around the parish.

Both sisters certainly 'fell in love' with the sick people they were caring for and were saddened when moved from this work. Unfortunately, both sisters were withdrawn from the parish because of other needs within the order. This situation brought a sadness to both sisters; the change in plans was both sudden and unexpected. It was also a sadness for the old people for whom they had been caring.

Getting serious about prayer In 1978 Sister Marie from the Blessed Sacrament Sisters began her prayer meetings in the parish centre. Sister Marie was transferred to Sydney, and her place was taken by Sister Maureen. The sisters were unable to continue the weekly groups, but the prayer continued with Sister Bernadette taking the lead.

The development of the prayer groups was exciting and came from a chance opportunity. Would we be prepared to try and see what happened? It was a beautiful ministry brought to our parish by the Sisters of the Blessed Sacrament.

Parish councils

Parish councils came into the life of the church in the 1960s and provided an opportunity for a priest to work with lay people in a shared mission. My first experience of a parish council was at Sandringham in those early days after the Vatican Council. Father Kelly was keen to get a parish council up and firing. Various parish meetings were arranged. In those days, around 1968, this concept of council was 'new stuff' for our people. We all had a lot to learn about the council role, both priests and laity.

It was a good experience to be there for the election of the first council at Sandringham. This new group of people were great; although, with all due respect, this new form of delegation was not the main strength of either Father Kelly or Father Scarborough. But that was alright. They had both chalked up many years of priestly ministry under a different expectation model.

At Glenhuntly, this sort of model was totally foreign to Father Paddy Gleeson. After all, he had completed almost fifty years of priesthood, all in parish life, and had never been expected to work with such a committee structure. But he was not lacking in initiative. When he had to send the cathedral details of his parish council, he simply put down the names of his own little 'core group'—that small band of men with whom he worked!

The early days of the parish council in Glenhuntly were spent in clarifying the role of the lay person in this model . . . and also clarifying the role of the priest!. One of the first things Father Paddy Gleeson asked of me was to establish a parish council. It took about eighteen months to get around to this, but eventually we formed a steering committee and reached election time. The parish council was duly elected and installed at a parish Mass on the Sunday. During that week I left for holidays.

Before leaving for holiday, I spent time with the newly elected chairman of our first parish council, Rolly Briglia. We outlined a plan for while I was away. I suggested that if possible, the councillors should meet three times to work out what they saw as their role as the parish council in Glenhuntly and to prioritise some of the parish needs. If they wanted something concrete to get themselves into action, they could look at establishing a parish credit society. I explained to Rolly that for almost a year I had been planning to establish a credit society, but I thought I would wait until the parish council had been established and let them take it over.

On returning from holidays, I was invited to a parish council gathering to hear the fruits of their discussions while I was away. They had certainly done a lot of work about their role and the needs which had to be faced. When Rolly finished outlining what they had done, I asked, 'What about the establishment of the credit society, Rolly?' Rolly simply answered, 'Well Father, we discussed that and felt it was not a priority for us at the moment, so we aren't going to do anything about it for the time being'. I immediately responded, 'Hey, wait a minute, I was going to establish this months ago but decided to leave it go for you mob'. Rolly replied, 'Father, you asked us to think about our role and prioritise the needs and that's what we decided'. Then I was able to say very sincerely, 'Thank you, Rolly'.

That was an important time in my own development of working with lay people in parish council or any other form of structure. Lay people are not to be seen simply as helpers of the parish priest, but rather people taking up their own role of ministry. If we are to make lay people responsible, then they must be responsible for their decisions.

I recall sharing this moment with an older parish priest friend of mine whose reply was, 'Well, you had better make them see that it is a priority!' I guess that's the sort of attitude we have legitimately held in the past but which has no place in the present.

Establishing a role for lay people When I arrived in the parish of Yarraville in 1975, there had been a council established for some years. However, there had not been elections for a few years and not a great deal was happening through the council. There was a lack of interest by the parishioners at large, a lack of enthusiasm within the council itself and certainly a lack of decision making and responsibility. In this regard, Yarraville may not have been vastly different to some other parishes around Melbourne.

At the end of 1976 an election was held. People were nominated and voted into the council. A new start was made. This was to be a most important group in the next few years.

If a parish council was really going to assume the role as outlined by the Vatican Council, the people themselves needed to understand this role. This would involve education and formation, and a growing in appreciation of the important ministry which was theirs as lay people in the Church.

In 1977 we set out together on a formation programme that was to lead the councillors to a growing realisation of their own individual mission in the Church and their corporate mission as a council.

The first discussion night looked at 'the Church'. We started from an image of the Church as a ghetto, perhaps a bit exaggerated. We moved to the image of a Church reaching out and meeting people wherever their needs were. The theme was called 'Mission or Maintenance', a title stolen from a book by Father Michael Winter. The title itself was a challenge to us. That first night was so important. People were honestly expressing some of their past experiences of church, and their hopes for the Church today. They shared these thoughts so easily with each other. It was a successful start to our programme of formation.

The next month we looked at 'The World in which we live'. Here we were helped by an article in the daily newspaper entitled 'Is there a God out West?'. In this article, the retiring Archbishop Woods expressed his regret that the Anglican church had not reached the people of the western suburbs of Melbourne. The many pressing needs of people were highlighted in the article. There was more than enough to pose many questions about the relevance and role of the Church in the lives of people in this area. Such a night could have become a disaster with an attitude of giving up in the face of so many questions. But not for this group, this was a challenge to be met by the Church.

And then came the great night, 'Why a Parish Council?' As a preparation for this night, each councillor answered three questions beforehand. What is the main purpose of a parish council? Why did you offer yourself for election? What are the urgent areas for the council at the moment?

There was plenty of discussion which culminated in the councillors themselves arriving at a definition of a parish council. The definition was their own. Here is what they decided.

> The Parish Council is a group of representative and concerned
> people who assume with the priests a shared responsibility for
> the mission of the Church in a particular area. It is therefore
> not a matter of assisting the clergy but rather of assuming a
> responsibility.

It's a powerful statement. The council referred back to this
statement on several occasions on later discussion nights. I'm
sure this night was one of the keys to establishing and main-
taining an effective parish council in Yarraville.

The following meetings took up some of the areas
considered by the councillors to be urgent. One of the first
concerns was the spiritual needs of people. There was a good
discussion on prayer. One of the councillors asked a leading
question, 'Instead of talking about prayer, should we be
praying too?' So we did! A whole new dimension to our
discussions was opened. The prayer and sharing helped meld
us into a closer group of people. Then we discussed questions
such as the needs of the elderly by using Scripture, prayers
and music in a reflective way.

It may seem that I am painting a rosy picture. There were
also a few times when interest was down, the discussions
didn't really work, even numbers were down occasionally.
But the council kept at it and it did work. There was a change
of councillors each year, but the unity continued through the
changes.

Management roles for lay people in St Kilda

Things are a bit different in St Kilda. We have not had a
parish pastoral council in the normal sense, but the principles
of lay people taking responsibility has always been present.

Given that our staff today is over fifty people, our welfare
budget is $1.5 million, Government contracts are involved and
a variety of ministries are carried out, something different is
needed in management structure. At present there is a Board

of Management which includes an executive of three parishioners who meet with the two priests, while a further seven parishioners form the board and meet each two months. Each of these seven board members heads a committee of management for the various ministries undertaken in St Kilda. The fourteen team co-ordinators also meet with the parish priest fortnightly. The 'How' of meetings is not important. It's the 'Why' which really matters. The purpose is sharing responsibility—lay people taking greater responsibility for their church.

There have been a host of management models for the Mission over the last eleven years as the Mission has grown. Things change from year to year and the model has to suit the time and the situation.

Parish team in St Kilda

From 1982, we have endeavoured to live and work as a team and to maintain a spirit of team ministry. A core group comprised of four or five people from the Mission team has met with me over the past few years, supporting and working with me in the day-to-day decisions which need to be made. As with the management structure of the Mission, the 'Why' of team meetings has top priority.

Team ministry brings a whole new dimension of support and affirmation for a priest. Sharing responsibility and decision making in a working situation brings with it a new sense of accountability. With this comes a new level of satisfaction and fulfilment as a priest working in community.

Similarly, sharing one's life in a living situation brings with it a different set of responsibilities to 'normal' presbytery living. Along with the responsibility comes joy and support in everyday living.

CHAPTER 8

Liturgy and Life

Liturgy—Celebrating Life

At the seminary, we came face to face with the word
'LITURGY' almost immediately. There was one expression
that I remember which makes sense to me: **Liturgy is life**.
I'm not sure that we could classify some of our liturgy as
having or celebrating life. Life doesn't necessarily mean the
way in which things are celebrated, although this is important.
To me, liturgy means the life situations of our world and our
people which give the keynote for celebration.

Back in the seminary, we were trained in a certain way to
celebrate the liturgy. We were taught about rubrics or rules in
a strict way which often gave incredible importance to the
'how' of things. For many priests, it is not easy to shake off
this attitude.

The same is true of preaching. During my first appointment
I began to write out sermons and file them away, being
assisted by Father Jack Kelly to have an orderly approach to
instructing the people. He had a series of sermon topics
worked out for the first few months, and I tried to follow it.

But I felt this was hopeless. I found myself speaking in the manner which I thought the people expected! I was wrong.

I threw away this sort of series and preparation and started to speak about life—my life, their lives, the world. I began to speak in my own style which I know is too fast and sometimes all over the place. But the one redeeming feature to this approach is that it forces you to speak from your heart. I often told stories at Sandringham, many about my own struggles, and Father Kelly gave me a warning, 'You're telling them too much about yourself, Smithy, and that's dangerous'.

John Price, the first chairman of the parish council and a former Anglican minister, said to me one day, 'You know, the way you preach annoys me. You break all the rules we were taught. You speak too quickly, you wander around, you have little asides and you use slang. And the people love it'. So I guess that I am just myself when I preach.

All this is saying that liturgy is life. Life to be enjoyed and celebrated. Life of the world to be brought into our liturgy. Life to be shared.

Secular holidays In the days of learning things by heart, the holy days of obligation included New Year's Day. The world celebrates New Year's Day. But the Church celebrated the Feast of the Circumcision. This was changed and we now have the Solemnity of Mary, the Mother of God. But the fact remains that it is New Year's Day so let's celebrate it!

I've always, except for the first couple of years, celebrated the Mass for New Year's Day as the opportunity to thank God for the past year and to ask the blessing of God on the year ahead. To miss out on this opportunity is to miss out on the life of the world and the people who have come together to celebrate. Perhaps the closing hymn should be 'Auld Lang Syne', with the chance to join hands together expressing our friendship and sense of unity and community and wishes of well being for each other.

I first sang 'Auld Lang Syne' as a hymn in Glenhuntly parish, and it has been quite a moving moment for me each year since. Somehow, this song is special to people, whatever and however its origin. During this New Year's Day Mass, I have led the people in a reflection of thanksgiving for the past year. This has meant picking out a few highlights, big events and small moments, in my own life. I usually have done this under a few headings. Of course it is impossible to cover a whole year in a few minutes, but the main point is to focus our attention on the ways in which God has walked with us over the past year. For many people in our congregation who live alone, this celebration has an added dimension because it provides 'family' for this special day or night. New Year's Day is real, so let's celebrate it.

The same thing can be said for Mother's Day and Father's Day. We can legitimately claim that these days are being over-commercialised, but they are nevertheless real in our world. They are happening. And they do give us the opportunity to reflect in thanksgiving on the gift of motherhood and fatherhood, to pray for parents, to recognise their place in our lives. Bringing these world 'moments' into our liturgical life doesn't take too much, and it doesn't need to be anything enormous. But the main point is not to ignore what the 'world' is celebrating. Over the last few years we have been naming our own 'Mother of the Year', in St Kilda.

On Anzac Day, we have another opportunity, but we also have the feast of St Mark the evangelist. While the 'world' is celebrating one event, up until recently we were celebrating something else—the feast day of St Mark. Not that there is anything wrong with St Mark, after all he did give us one of the Gospels. When there is something special happening outside our church building, we also need to be part of it.

There are special Masses available for such occasions and it doesn't take a great deal of effort to obtain the flag and the tape of the 'Last Post' from the local undertaker. The time of reverence and silence is important and brings us in touch with the 'world' outside.

Prayer—a sign of love

Prayer is a sign of love. When I think of the really top class 'pray-ers' whom I have known, I feel that love is the key to their prayer. Perhaps the lesson is that the more we love, the better we can be prayerful people.

Prayer in a formal sense has never been my forte. I've never been a great one for being organised and consistent in this or that spiritual or prayerful area. I recalled earlier, that in seminary I came to the shocking realisation that prayer was for life, not just the eight years.

My own prayer life has been a mixed bag. I've made lots of sensible decisions and resolutions about prayer. Most of those have lasted for a while at least. I'm good at resolutions in times of spiritual fervour. I have hung in there, sometimes feeling close to God in silent prayer, while at other times I've been just a bit too busy or too tired. I've always been good at excuses too!

One encouragement I received in seminary days came from Father Austin Ryan, a down-to-earth sort of priest. One of his axioms was that the first and most important thing about prayer was 'Be there!' With morning meditation in those seminary days, that was about all I could manage. Knowing just how I have to struggle to be 'on the job' with prayer, I could never attempt to judge how well people were praying. It's enough for me that opportunities are there for people to be in touch with the Lord in prayer.

However, I can still say that I have had some wonderful times of prayer. Generally these moments have been with other people because I am not good by myself.

Finding opportunities for times of prayer In Yarraville, there were a variety of ways in which prayer came into the pastoral life of the parish. It seemed that there need be no limit to the ways and the times of prayer for people once our eyes had been opened.

In the beginning, annual days of prayer were introduced for the ladies of the parish, usually with a guest priest to lead the day. Then the parish council began prayer reflection evenings on a monthly basis. The team headed off now and again for times of prayer. Prayer groups were introduced to the parish by the Blessed Sacrament Sisters.

As recalled earlier, the parish council came upon the matter of prayer through a discussion night. Instead of talking about prayer, we decided that we should in fact be praying. We took the topic for discussion and handled it in a prayerful context of Scripture, music, quiet and prayer. This atmosphere gave a new thrust to the discussions. Over time, we grew to be more comfortable with nights of prayer and shared some impressive spiritual experiences together.

The same approach took place with the Welfare Committee which met every two months. This was a group made up of representatives from the various parish caring groups. At these nights the leader of the group would prepare prayers as reflections on our work. Reports and experiences of the past two months were shared in a prayerful context.

The team of people working together in Yarraville always found time for getting away for a time of prayer. There could be reasons for not getting away, but we still made it. At Easter and Christmas things could be particularly busy, but at these times we also managed to find that space for prayer together.

I remember a parish priest coming to see me in Yarraville to find out what was happening. We were talking about the prayer 'things' in the parish. Eventually I told him about the parish council prayer nights. At this point he said, 'Even the council prays? You've killed me now, Smithy!'

This same spirit has been present in St Kilda. When I arrived in 1982, there was a First Friday time of adoration which gave a prayerful quiet time before the Blessed Sacrament. Here was a good opportunity. So a First Friday day of prayer was introduced. A roster similar to the old days of 'Forty Hours Devotion' was set up with at least one person for each section of time throughout Friday. The message to the parishioners was that the way for the parish to respond to the needs of the world would be through a prayer base. We still have adoration on the First Friday of each month for an hour after Mass or Communion service at each of our two churches.

Prayer groups   There have been a variety of developments in prayer groups for people over recent years in the Catholic Church, so there's nothing so special about what I want to share. However, in Yarraville we tried to reach out to the 'ordinary' people in the parish—people who would not normally be attracted to an organised prayer group.

In 1978, by absolute chance, or more likely divine providence, a great opportunity came our way. I was at the Blessed Sacrament Sisters convent to collect some altar breads. I often visited the convent for a quiet time in their grounds by myself, so I knew the sisters. This day, they were actually discussing Yarraville parish and the possibility of the sisters becoming involved in assisting people with prayer. In a matter of weeks, Sister Marie began the prayer groups in Yarraville.

Each Tuesday, Sister Marie conducted two sessions at the parish centre—in the morning from 10–12 a.m., and in the afternoon from 1–3 p.m. There were four groups of people who met once a month in the morning—the drivers for the special Mass for the elderly, the members of the Catholic Family Welfare Bureau auxiliary, the parish team and a general group. In the afternoon there were two groups of mothers from the playgroup and each group met fortnightly.

At these prayer times, the ladies were given the chance for a time of quiet, a few thoughts for meditation from Sister Marie, and an introduction to various ways of prayer and contemplation. I took part myself and found that I could tackle forms of prayer, such as breathing in prayer using simple phrases. The atmosphere itself was encouraging to all of us. The time spent in prayer not only helped the individuals, but it also enhanced the particular works in which they were engaged together. Bonds between individuals were strengthened. Twelve years later, one of those groups is still going.

In St Kilda, with the assistance of Sister Irene from the Presentation Sisters Prayer Centre, similar attempts have been made to offer prayer time for the 'ordinary' parishioner—that person who is always at mass, can be depended upon to give a hand and goes to parish functions. Sister Irene took small groups of people and conducted a 'home retreat' in which they gathered once a week for a few months. They were given their prayer programme to take home for the week. This opportunity has been appreciated by the people.

This programme of 'home retreat' for the regularly involved parishioners has been continued, and people have been invited back for 'refresher days'. These opportunities have a life impact on people. The notion of prayer is opened up for the people with new dimensions and new understanding. I would like to believe that their prayer truly is a reflection of their love for the world.

The chapel—A place of peace I came home from overseas in 1979 with a resolution gained from my experiences while away. I felt that a chapel was more important for me than a bedroom, so on my return I converted my little bedroom in our Yarraville house into a chapel. I bought a divan, which converted to a bed at night, in my office. The chapel was a bit rough and small, but it gave a place of quiet and peacefulness for me and any visitors to the house. I can recall some delightful moments about the chapel. Perhaps by sharing some of these with you, the spirit of this move will become more apparent.

On one occasion, a man came to see me about a few worries and, after a bit of a talk, I suggested he should spend a few minutes in the chapel. He didn't come out, so after about an hour, I wandered in to him. He looked at me and said, 'I'm sorry, Father, do I have to go now?' Obviously the answer was for him to stay a bit longer. I'm sure that for this man, this was perhaps the first time for a long while that he had the chance to simply sit quietly and peacefully in the presence of the Father.

Sister Bernadette was in a flurry one day when I arrived home. This young couple were in a state. The young woman wanted to kill herself. Sister Bernadette was trying to keep her calm. The woman had settled down in the chapel. I went to have a chat with her there. She made it obvious that she wasn't having any of this 'religious stuff' and didn't want to be here anyway. I was getting nowhere fast and suggested that I might say a prayer for her. She didn't care one way or another, so I launched into a couple of simple prayers and a bit of Scripture. After this, she asked whether she could have a smoke. She took out her cigarettes, but then decided that she didn't feel right to be smoking in this place. What was happening was that she was becoming more peaceful.

Eventually she asked to spend time alone in the chapel. She went home at peace. I'm sure that the quiet prayerful atmosphere of the chapel had been a great help to her.

Having a chapel on the premises at Yarraville meant that we were a bit spoiled. With a prayerful chapel only yards away, prayer times were somewhat more accessible. For those of us working at the parish centre, it was a source of spiritual strength. When we changed houses at the end of 1980, the new house didn't have a small room to convert into a chapel. By now, we knew that a chapel was an essential part of our centre so we divided the lounge with a little wall and there was our chapel. The new parish centre was then complete.

In St Kilda there was a chapel in the presbytery even before the building became the 'Mission House'. During those early days when there were just a few of us living or working in St Kilda, we had times of prayer together in the chapel.

There have been some short periods when the chapel has been lost because we haven't had enough room for the people working at the Mission. However, the chapel keeps coming back. It's so important to have that place of peace and quiet. Over the years visitors have been welcome to spend time in the chapel. As the Mission House has become busier and more populated with offices and people, a place of quiet is harder to find. But we still have the chapel area.

Reflection days

Just up the street from the Sacred Heart Mission is the Prayer Centre of the Presentation Sisters. The building was originally used as a small school, but in recent years it has been renovated into a beautiful and peaceful building. It is set in a delightful garden. Over the years we have been blessed with opportunities for times of reflection, sometimes conducted by Sister Irene and at other times managed by ourselves. This peaceful prayerful environment has been a great asset to the Mission.

The reflection days for our Mission House volunteers have been well attended and appreciated. On most of these occasions, I have led the days which has been a rewarding experience. The Mission team has also spent a full day of prayer together on many occasions. Special visitors to the Mission such as Brother Andrew from India, Edwina Gately from Chicago and the Basic Christian Community's formation team from Latin America, have all conducted times of prayer and sharing at the Centre.

The very presence of a man such as Brother Andrew was sufficient in itself for a reflection day. His simple manner of speaking and sharing of life and values was a wonderful experience. Edwina Gately worked with women in Chicago who were involved in a life of prostitution, drugs and homelessness. Using her life experiences as a base, she led parishioners in a day of reflection which examined our attitudes to our world and people who live on the fringe of society. The team from South America were brilliant. They moved people to a broad understanding of a world church through various exercises and reflections which were backed up with a host of delightful stories.

A special prayer   The Sacred Heart Mission was set up officially in 1983 and the first executive committee was established. Our first annual meeting of the Sacred Heart Mission was held in the parish hall late in 1984. This was a big day. On this occasion we presented to the parishioners and supporters our 'Mission Prayer'. Cath Stewart had put the prayer together and both the team and executive had discussed it. The final official prayer was said by everyone present.

The 'Mission Prayer' is said at every team meeting, at every executive meeting, at public gatherings of the Mission such as the Annual Meeting and at various other group meetings. I would also feel confident saying that many people, parishioners and supporters say our Mission prayer on a regular basis.

Mission Prayer

Father, we ask Your blessing on our life and work here at Sacred Heart Mission. In faith, we recognise that You are the Creator of all people, and that You have given us a share in Your creative love.

We are thankful that You have made us in the image of Christ who reaches into the depth of our lives. As Christ gathers us together and dwells in the midst of our community, He teaches us how to share His forgiveness and love with all people, especially those who are in need of His trust and hope.

Your spirit gives us life to bear witness to Christ's mission, calling all people to freedom, justice, dignity and love.

Together in Your name, we pray that we may always walk in the friendship of Christ, and give to all people Your blessing of peace.

God's sacraments

At a seminar for priests a few years ago, a discussion went on about marriage and our role in getting serious about the preparation. We didn't want people just using the sacraments without full understanding. The resolutions began to come forth, and before you know what's happening, a set of guidelines are being drawn up. At that point, I stood up and made a response in the vein of 'With the guidelines for Communion, I would never have been eligible to receive the Eucharist; with the guidelines for Baptism, my parents would have been knocked back for my Baptism; I would have had trouble getting into a Catholic school—and now, with these guidelines being proposed, you wouldn't even *marry* my parents. Surely we've got to leave a bit of room for God's grace to work, because after all is said and done, they are God's sacraments'.

I suppose that my own family experience makes me aware that the sacraments do belong to God. After all, my parents were not practical Catholics. If they were approaching a priest today, they may well strike a tough reception. The same could be true about Baptism, First Communion and Confirmation for my sister and me. They didn't attend Mass and didn't worry too much if we did not attend. But somehow, grace must have been at work.

I was approached by a young man in Glenhuntly parish about his mother wanting to be baptised a Catholic. This rather surprised me because he and his mother were always at Mass. What unfolded was a fascinating story about the sacraments.

When this lady was having her first child, there were complications and she was in danger of losing her life. She heard the doctors discussing her situation and whether they could save both the baby and her. She said a prayer to God and promised that if the baby were born safely, she would give him back to God. Then she passed out. When she awoke, both she and the baby were all right. Great joy.

Some time later she remembered her promise and thought about how she could give the child back to God. Well, baptism at least, so she considered the churches and felt that the Catholic Church looked the best. So off to the church she went with her story. She approached St Colmans Church in Balaclava (this was around 1950), and she asked the parish priest, Father Bill Mangan, if he would baptise her little boy. And he did! Later on, her second son was born and baptised at the same Church. She then raised them as Catholics through Catholic schools.

The big day came when her oldest boy came to her and said, 'Mum, I've got a big surprise for you. I want to join the Christian Brothers'. Needless to say, she was not surprised because this was the boy she promised to give back to God!

We had a private ceremony at home when both the parents were received into the Catholic church during a Mass. Not too long later the mother became sick and died.

Sometimes it takes a story such as this one to remind us that grace is given how and where God pleases. The sacraments are but one of God's channels of grace.

In Yarraville, we had a special baptism of Rebecca. She had been literally left at the hotel by her mother for awhile, but the while went on indefinitely. Then the lady who ran the hotel decided that she would keep the baby herself. In fact, she went on to adopt the baby. Well, Irene wanted the baby baptised and a date was duly arranged. When it came time for the Baptism on the Sunday afternoon, a large crowd was gathered. These were all the regular customers from the hotel who knew all about Rebecca and her situation. This was their baby Becky. At the time of welcoming the child into the community with the Sign of the Cross on the forehead, everyone was invited to come forward. This baby, who at the time had no immediate family, had a large family to welcome her into the church. Afterwards it was back to the pub for the reception. Beer was on the house, prawns were there in abundance and an enormous spread was laid out. It was a great party!

St Kilda has given us the opportunity to have great celebrations of baptism. The preparation may sometimes be a bit ragged, but the event itself, that's a different matter.

One of the families wanted to arrange a baptism for two children, aged seventeen and thirteen. It had to be soon because the godparents would be going to court and they would probably be 'away' for quite awhile—in prison. What was really needed in this case—guidelines or welcome? After a time of preparation, the day arrived. It was seen as important by the family, many of whom were caught up in the crime scene. My most vivid memory of the day was the noise in the church as I was filling in the baptismal book in the sacristy. I looked around the door and saw that a game of hide and seek was on, but it was some of the adults who were making the most noise. I'm sure God has a sense of humour on such occasions!

Margaret Payne was in a house of special accommodation, meaning that she needed supported living. Whenever Communion services were held at the home, Margaret would attend until, one day, she decided to become a Catholic. Margaret was almost eighty-five years old. A special home Mass was arranged and the elderly Catholic folk gathered. I was going to put Margaret through a test and they could decide whether or not I should let her into our church. I put some tough questions to her. Did she believe in God? Jesus Christ? Holy Communion? and prayer? Would she try to be good? She answered 'Yes' to them all and everyone agreed that she had done well with the answers. We welcomed Margaret into the Church during that home Mass. Margaret came second in the 'age stakes' because earlier that same year Gus Herzel received a special welcome into our community at the age of eighty-six.

Old Gus lived in the block of flats just down the road from the church. Night after night he would walk to the Fitzroy Street shops for his evening meal. Often we would stand outside the Mission House chatting away. In the process we became good friends. Sometimes he would call into the church and say a prayer. Then one day he said to me that he would like to become a part of our church. He was duly 'instructed' and during a Sunday Mass we welcomed him into our community. This was one of the most moving receptions into the church community. As this stooped, old man with a walking stick came up to the front of the altar and gave his assent, there were more than a few tears being shed in the church.

Margaret Zorz wanted to become a Catholic. I had celebrated the marriage of her daughter Tanya a couple of years before. Shortly afterwards, Margaret had been found to have cancer, and I had visited her in the hospital. Now she had been diagnosed as having terminal cancer. She felt that she had a bit of a cheek wanting to enter the Church at this late stage. I assured her that she wasn't too late so 'Jump up on the cart!' I saw Margaret a couple of times for a long chat. She wanted to join four other adult people who were to be received into our church just before Christmas. Everything was set, but on that particular day Margaret was too ill to attend the church. During the week I suggested to her husband that we could have a private ceremony at home, but Margaret would have nothing of that. On the following Sunday, a few days before Christmas, Margaret attended Mass and was received into our community. This was special to us and to Margaret. The congregation knew of Margaret's situation because she was on our 'prayer list'. We celebrated an emotional reception into our community. Margaret died within the month, but with additional peace and strength gained through the sacraments.

Christmas carols

One of the highlights of enjoyment is our parish Carols Night. The style of this celebration started in Sandringham, but I have adapted this style over the years, putting the emphasis on family celebration. The pageant presented by the youth, a choir, youth on guitars and drums and old favourites sung by the congregation. The same ingredients are at any carols evening, but there is something extra which I feel that we have. Fun! Yes, even in the church.

Father Kelly introduced me to carols. In fact, the presbytery reeked of carols for the weeks before Christmas. He had an enormous library of tapes and records with Christmas carols from all around the world. I remember once that I heard a carol on the radio called 'One Star'. I rang to enquire about it and was told that it was on a record not being issued in Australia. When I explained why I wanted it, they made a special tape for me. Father Kelly thought it was nice and worked out the music and words so that we could have it in our church for Christmas.

On another occasion, I brought home with me from New Zealand a record from Argentina, courtesy of the MacDougall clan. It had some beautiful songs, but they were all in Spanish! The record cover had an English translation which I adapted to the music. One of the singers in Yarraville, Maryanne Charles, worked out the music from the record. This became one of my favourite Christmas carols called 'This is the Night'.

Christmas 1980 was a special event at Yarraville. The format for the Carols Night was changed somewhat from previous years and the focus was on 'gift'. People were invited to bring their gift to the child in the crib. These gifts centered around music. We listened to 84-year-old Jim

Robertson play 'Amazing Grace' on his bagpipes as he walked the full length of the aisle. This was the first of the gifts and set the tone for a beautiful celebration. Bess Kilgore, at eighty-three, played the organ and placed the music sheet before the crib scene. The crib scene was, as always, 'live' and presented by the youth. Claude Campbell, having only one arm, played 'The Holy City' on the trumpet and placed his instrument before the crib; drums, guitar, violin, piano accordion and a solo song all followed. Finally, Tony Fiorenza and Minna McGuire danced before the crib with a presentation specially arranged to express praise by two professional dancers. It was a memorable night, beautifully presented, but it still kept the atmosphere of joy and relaxation and 'being at home' in the church. It could easily have become a concert or performance, but it remained a night of joy in participation. On these special nights we have an experience of happiness within our parish family which gives reason for thanksgiving.

Last Christmas, we decided to have a Christmas Carols evening in our church which could perhaps appeal to the 96 per cent of people who don't generally frequent any church in St Kilda. It was to be a 'missionary' effort to take the message of Christmas out from the church. We did this by putting leaflets advertising the evening in the letter boxes of all the houses and flats in the vicinity.

The next task was to determine the format for the evening.

St Kilda is recognised as one of the art and theatre centres for people. So the night would focus on the gift of the performing arts. It was to be local artists sharing their gifts with the people.

The entire sanctuary became the setting for a crib scene arranged by adults taking part. This was not to be a children's show, but an adult presentation. Among the shepherds and kings were some of the Board of Management along with other parishioners. The pageant was impressive and solemn.

The items presented before the crib included a string quartet, a couple of solo items from singers, a children's story read by a television personality and an organ recital. Several people brought forward works of art and craft. Gifts were presented, shared and recognised on this night. A good night was had by all. More important, people had responded to the invitation. Hopefully this 'reaching out' evening will continue to touch the lives of more people.

There have been many variations on this theme of a Christmas Carol celebration over the years I have spent in Sandringham, Glenhuntly, Yarraville and now St Kilda. I love these nights! They are about family, joy, the time of year, peace and hope. Our parish family is at a celebration.

Over the last twenty years our church has moved dramatically in the celebration of the Eucharist and the other sacraments. There has been increased involvement of lay people, a great variety in the use of music, development of symbols, rearrangement of church seating and fittings, innovative architecture—the list could go on.

We have been given the opportunity as a community of Christians gathered around the altar to celebrate our faith together. The challenge is perhaps to hold on to the word 'celebration'. It is a word which must evoke an image of 'life'. That's where I began and will end this chapter—Liturgy is life.

CHAPTER 9

Fun in Community Life

At a national youth conference in Canberra, I was asked to arrange the special Mass for the students and chaplains gathered from all over Australia. The Mass was arranged for 9 p.m., which is not the best time in the world for a celebration of life. I was then told that Bishop Carroll was coming from Wagga. He would be the principal celebrant. The question then was how to have a joyful celebration with a bishop as main celebrant?

I came across Bishop Carroll by chance at the evening meal. Coming to his table, I saw a priest whom I had not previously met. I introduced myself by saying 'Ernie Smith from Melbourne'. He responded with 'Bishop Carroll from Wagga'. I then told him I had some good news and some bad news for him. Which would he like first? He wanted the good news. So I replied, 'There's a Mass on tonight and you're the main celebrant'. He then asked what the bad news was. I hastened to inform him of the bad news; I was the organiser of the Mass. He asked what the theme was and I told him, 'Being happy in the circus'. The main question at issue was, as I put it to him, 'Are you happy being a bishop?'

He assured me that he was, and I asked him to tell all at the Mass why he was happy being a bishop.

He gave a great sermon about being happy as a bishop. He gave an interesting parallel that has stuck with me ever since. He felt that often people who were fanatics about causes, whether in the church or in the world, seemed to be very serious about life. Most fanatics, he noticed, were not very joyful people. As people committed to the Church, we were expected to be 'fanatics' for the cause of Christ. However, as the message of Christ is bringing the Good News to the world, we should always aim to be 'joyful fanatics'.

I believe that the phrase 'joyful fanatic' highlights an important part of our life as Christians. We must be people of joy, because the message we carry is one of joy. As a poster hanging around our Mission says, in the words of Teilhard de Chardin, 'Joy is an infallible sign of the presence of God'. That is a powerful statement. I like it. On the negative side it means that if there is no joy, then that's not how God likes it. This joy is not necessarily about laughter and smiling, but about that deep joy which cannot be taken away.

If we are truly joyful people, we will have lots of lovely moments to remember and share—the times when we have felt deep happiness with other people, the times when our world has been filled with genuine laughter, the times of fun. This joy must be an attitude, a way of life for the Christian. Deep joy can never be taken away by the sadness of certain situations, the tragedies of daily life or the struggles of people. Somehow Christian joy must always be present.

Fun concerts Concerts and entertainment have generally been part of my life as a priest. Perhaps I have an unfulfilled desire to be on the stage! Over my years of priesthood I have always enjoyed working with people, particularly young people and children, in parish concerts and fun nights.

There is a little bit of the fool in all of us. Perhaps in some more than others, so maybe I have received more than my share of 'fool'. In parish concerts over the years, as well as being Master of Ceremonies, I have been involved in several 'fool' roles. Hearing an audience rocking with laughter or clapping with appreciation is a nice feeling. Our concerts have given the people the chance for both of these expressions of joy.

There have been some excellent presentations of music and song by both the primary school children and the youth groups. They have been enjoyed by the audience and by the singers. Enjoyed is the operative word, even if this has sometimes meant an 'amateur' production. Concerts were times for fun and relaxation for everyone. The comedy side of the concert is always a big hit. I usually managed to have a role. Why I score the villain roles in the melodramas I don't know. Perhaps it gives the people a legitimate chance to boo the priest!! One year I shed the role of villain when I was given the role of the fairy godmother in a Cinderella comedy.

Why play the fool in this way? Because we are a family at play. We are having fun. I enjoy having fun with people. The concerts in Sandringham, Glenhuntly, Yarraville and St Kilda have always been times of fun for the entire family. They have helped to build our parish family.

We staged a parish concert in Sandringham. One of the highlights was *The Poor Little Mill Girl*, an old-fashioned fruity melodrama that had a cast of six men from the parish, including myself. We listed the six actors in order of appearance, without giving away which role they would play. When I appeared on the stage in my role, it brought the house down. My role was that of Lucy, the unfortunate mill girl. I appeared resplendent in a tattered dress, stockings with gaping holes, unsightly boots and a stringy wig. I had to wait for a long time before I could successfully get out my opening words. We had some lovely fun evenings in Sandringham. The same pattern of concerts was repeated in Glenhuntly parish.

Although this fun cannot be in every aspect of parish life, the place of joyfulness must pervade every activity. Joy is a sign of God. Joy is a gift and should be present in our parish life.

'Music on Wheels' When I was at Glenhuntly, I read an article in the daily paper about a couple of entertainers, Coral Gunning and Maree Gaye, who were in Melbourne giving concerts. They had set up an organisation in Adelaide called 'Music on Wheels', the idea being that if people could not get out of their homes, they would arrange a personal concert at home for them. What a simple and beaut idea. I rang and asked them about putting on a bit of a concert for some old people in Glenhuntly parish. They agreed and we had a lovely day.

What I didn't realise was that I was being caught up with their work, just as I have a bit of a habit of involving others when they come along to see me. I found myself involved in setting up a Melbourne branch of 'Music on Wheels'.

A group of us met and talked about the idea; before long we were up and going. Through music, I met some wonderful people. Not being a singer or musician myself, my job became compere and fill-in man. A list of entertainers was drawn up, and we started sending out little concert groups. Sometimes the request would be for a singer to give a few 'golden oldies' in a private home. On other occasions, a group of three or four would go to a hospital ward for chronic sufferers. We also went to special accommodation houses, many of them in St Kilda.

'Music on Wheels' had a focus on personal involvement of the people, so we had boxes of musical 'gadgets'—bells, whistles, big rattles, clackers, little cymbals, sticks to tap together—anything that made a noise and could be rattled in time with the musicians. It was great to see the people becoming animated through music and singing the old favourites.

Involvement meant that we also discovered quite a bit of hidden talent—a pianist who had not played for years, a singer who could still hit a note or two. We would take them on concerts to other sick people.

Unfortunately, the 'Music on Wheels' folded in Melbourne after a few years, but not before many of us had gained so much from the concerts. Music and fun shared by people.

Magic Over the years I had picked up a few magic tricks which I would keep in reserve for children's gatherings or elderly people's gatherings. The tricks were fairly basic, but they did the job of bringing joy to people. I also had a repertoire of games and stories for youth, that proved great hits.

Trips to New Guinea Mission trips can also be fun and rewarding as well. In those early years at Sandringham and Glenhuntly, I had the chance to share my experiences of New Guinea with some of the young people from these two parishes.

At the end of 1969, five young women from our youth group in Sandringham went off to help in the missions during the Christmas vacation period. The YCW group assisted with their preparation and raised some money for the trip. For each of the girls, it was a special experience, but for one in particular, Jenny Merrick, this was to change her life completely. During the following year, Jenny was in touch with Bishop Schmidt from Mendi diocese about the possibility of spending some years in the missions. Well, it happened. At the end of 1979, Jenny returned to Papua-New

Guinea to begin her four years at Ialibu in the southern highlands. But she didn't return alone. A party of fourteen of us headed off to the island for a working holiday, twelve of us going to Sissano.

Over several months, many events around the parish of Sandringham focussed on this trip. We raised money for the fares, collected goods for the missions, and planned very thoroughly for the trip. We were going to build two classrooms and an office for a school at this place called Sissano.

At Sissano, it was straight into the work. It was hot and sticky with mosquitoes and sandflies. It is definitely not the place to establish a holiday resort. This time was significant for this group of young people and, in some cases, had a life-long effect upon them.

In Glenhuntly, the opportunity was there for another big trip with twelve young people going away to Mendi diocese in the Southern Highlands. This time, the youth were scattered over four or five mission stations doing a wide variety of jobs for a few weeks.

Looking back, these mission trips were great times and meant so much to all the young people who took part. Above all else, they were fun times shared.

Football Another day I remember with a smile was the football match arranged at Sandringham between the YCW and the fathers. Considering myself to be a 'father', I said I would be playing on their side against the young people of the parish. I became the main target for the young people. As self-appointed coach of the 'fathers', I assured the fathers before the game that they need not worry about the young people trying to knock them down. The young people's main concern would be to flatten me, and I felt that I could successfully avoid them. What I didn't bank on was my own team. Throughout the game I kept an eagle eye on the opposition, making sure they couldn't bowl me over. I didn't reckon on one of my own team, namely recently ordained Father Dennis Minogue, running straight into me. He was wearing glasses which successfully cut my eye open and gave me an enormous black eye. After the game that Sunday evening I was scheduled to say the evening Mass. I walked onto the altar with a quite obvious closed and swollen black eye. I said nothing through the early part of the Mass, until the sermon. I then read out the parish notices, one of which said that on Sunday afternoon there would be a football match between the parents and the YCW boys. I looked straight at the congregation and said, 'The game has been played!' This brought the house down.

Preparing a meal In the early days of preparing meals in the hall, the lack of food resources could present a bit of a problem. But even the problem-solving became a bit of fun. On one occasion we were given several hundred tins of food. The only problem was that the tins were unlabelled! It was very much a case of chance as to what might be in the tins. We checked the numbers on each tin and put the same numbered tines together, so that if we opened one tin with a certain number we would at least know that all those tins were the same. In the hope of trying to find a tin of stew, we would often open a tin of apricots or a tin of jam or whatever. Eventually we managed to sort out all these tins into some sort of order and nothing ever went to waste. From the St Vincent de Paul Society we also received many tins of food. But we often wondered why so many people gave us 3 Bean Mix, 4 Bean Mix, 5 Bean Mix, and 7 Bean Mix. It seemed like nobody wanted the beans!

In those very early days of providing a meal, someone telephoned from Hamilton, in the country district of Victoria.

I was asked if we could do with twenty sheep. There was a drought on, and it wasn't worth the trouble for the farmers to take the sheep to market. They would kill them, cut them up, and bring them to us. I thought this was a tremendous gesture and readily accepted the offer. However, we discovered the difference between city and country terminology. For us in the city, 'cut up' meat meant legs of lamb, chops etc. For the person on the farm, 'cut up' meant cut up into four pieces. So on a Friday evening, twenty carcasses of sheep arrived.

I contacted a friend in Yarraville, Jim Bonello, who worked at a meat works. He arrived on Saturday, armed with his knives and choppers, and proceeded to instruct me and four or five other 'volunteers'. Then we dug into the task of chopping up these carcasses into legs of lamb, chops, flaps, soup bones and various other pieces. The kitchen of the presbytery was splattered with blood that day. It was an absolute mess. The end result was that we had bags and bags of meat to last us for meals in the hall for the next week or two. The process, well that was a different matter.

A joyful wake There's nothing like a good surprise to get a spirit of joy into a gathering. One such spontaneous party sprang from a sad occasion when we were gathered in the home of the Haynes family in Yarraville after the sudden death of Olga, the wife and mother of this family.

Sister Bernadette had recently come across an old meat mincer, so all the meat leftovers suddenly became converted into old-fashioned cottage pie. The talk at the home after the funeral drifted to cottage pie. Ted recalled how much he used to enjoy cottage pie, but hadn't had any for years. A couple of others remarked in a similar vein. Before you knew what had happened, a cottage pie party was arranged for the following week. By the end of the week, a good crowd of Ted's closest friends in the parish were coming to the cottage pie party.

A couple of days before the party, Sister Bernadette went around to the guests to collect the meat leftovers. The budget suffered when Sister Bernadette actually cooked a leg of lamb so that we could put it through the mincer! (For the uninitiated, cottage pie is made from a base of minced cooked meat, topped with potato, and then baked in the oven. It's an old-fashioned way of using the leftovers.)

About twenty people gathered a week after Olga's death to celebrate with cottage pie and tomato sauce. Surely a royal banquet! It was one of the happiest days in the parish centre, and yet it had grown out of tragedy and sadness. We had fun together, and in this case the joy was certainly a sign of the presence of God.

What was even more special was the fact that for the next couple of years, this cottage pie day became an annual event around the time of Olga's anniversary. I guess you could say it was a strange way to remember someone's anniversary, but then in another way, perhaps not.

Caring can be fun! There were some memorable 'fun times' in Yarraville with the refugee people from the nearby hostel.

Our first family get-together was a nervous day for our parish families. Each of the fourteen volunteer families was host to a refugee family. They were asked to provide enough food for their own family and their refugee family. When they arrived at the parish centre, all the food was placed on one table. With well over a hundred people at the gathering, there was quite a stack of food.

In preparation, the host families were given a list of 'who's who' for the day. This gave the names of their refugee family—Vietnamese, Laotian, or Cambodian—as these names would be correctly written in England. Alongside each name was a phonetic version. They were instructed to learn how to pronounce these names for the party. There were some real tongue-twisters. Most of the refugee people spoke little, if any English. It was a fun day as people did their best to communicate.

I hold one fascinating moment in my mind from this day. A Maltese lady was speaking about her grandchild to a Cambodian lady who also had a grandchild. They were each speaking in their own language. Each of them held their own grandchild on their lap and through the use of many gestures, they were actually understanding each other.

A lovely friendliness was always present at subsequent days, and communication was established in different ways. Children played games together and managed to make themselves understood. Our own youth brought out guitars at one of the parties. Before too long people had their chairs in circles around the guitar players. Our young people sang a few songs, the refugee young people sang a few songs, and people joined in whatever way they could, perhaps only by clapping.

For four years the Yarraville parish undertook responsibility for the 'Father Christmas' segment at the hostel party. We helped Father Christmas to provide toys for each child under twelve. I was the man of the day, Father Christmas. This was another parish fun day. Quite a few people from the parish became involved on these days. It's quite a job for Father Christmas to give presents to more than four hundred children. It's a big job to collect, sort, wrap and grade gifts for so many children. It's an even bigger job to keep order among so many children when Father Christmas arrives on the scene. A marvellous scheme was worked out the first year. Father Christmas would have helpers giving out presents. Not one child approached the clown or the fairy princess! The only person they wanted was Father Christmas. By the end of the festivity, the helpers had had enough for the day and Father Christmas was content to disappear until next year.

Laughter in the midst of sadness   Bill Blair had been around the place for some time.   He was a chronic alcoholic.   Now and again he would be on the straight and narrow for a few days or a week or even more, but inevitably he would break down again.   On this occasion he was ready to go to Mount Gambier to an alcohol rehabilitation centre.   He was full of fervour and enthusiasm.   To get Bill to Mount Gambier meant placing him on a bus in the city at 7.30 a.m.   I arranged with Bill, who was staying in one of our houses at the time, to collect him in the morning. I stressed that we must leave by 7 a.m.

When I arrived to collect him, he was snoring quite soundly.   The residents of the house had conducted a farewell party for Bill the night before because he was heading off to dry out.   I had to wake up Bill and get him on his feet so he could make it to the bus.   When I had him on his feet for awhile I realised that the snoring was still continuing from the bed. I pulled back the blankets to discover a young woman, also drunk, snoring her head off. I put the blankets back over and left her for the time being. I managed to get Bill on to the bus and off to Mount Gambier where he made a sensational recovery.

He arrived home some time later, a converted man. Bill, after seeing the light, now stated that he didn't drink, smoke, swear, gamble or go out with women. He became an absolute pain in the neck.   Bill had seen the light and was 'hot gospelling' to anybody in sight. I remember ringing Mount Gambier and speaking to the people in charge. Joking with them, I said, 'What the hell have you done to Bill? He's unbearable'. After about a week, Bill came to me with the news that he had just had a bet on a race. I rejoiced and said 'Welcome back, Bill, to the human race'.

This may sound flippant or light-hearted, but it's meant to give an indication of the many and varied ways the journey in alcoholism takes people. That was not the beginning of a new life for Bill. That came much later. Today Bill is married and in a regular job, living in a nice home in another suburb. He has made a new beginning. This stage was one of many points along the way. We had a lot of fun with Bill over the years.

Birthdays Birthdays are also special and a chance to celebrate. They are about loving and sharing life with others. It shouldn't be presumed that only people with sad and lonely lives miss out on birthdays. Not all families celebrate birthdays. I remember a priest (and they are generally not sad or alone) at a young child's birthday asking whether he could help the child to blow out the candles. Why? Because he had never blown out birthday cake candles.

We had a priest stay with us at Yarraville for a few months, and the young people decided to have a surprise birthday party for him. Unexpectedly, he decided to have a few days off on retreat, and this included his birthday. Not to be deterred, one of the young girls rang him at the retreat centre and pleaded that she desperately needed to speak to him. Of course he arranged to meet her on the evening of his birthday. When he duly arrived home in a most serious mood, to counsel this desperately worried young girl, he went into my office for privacy. Once he was securely closeted in my office, the young people appeared from everywhere with decorations, cakes and all that was needed for his birthday party. It took several knocks for him to answer and emerge from the office. He was greeted by a crowd of young people singing 'Happy Birthday'. A great moment. What we didn't expect were the tears from this priest because he couldn't remember his last birthday party.

It doesn't need to be a big show to be important. 'Joe' was a young fellow in Yarraville who came to the house most days for lunch and to do a bit of the gardening. He lived alone and life was a bit of a battle. The house was where he found friends, and so his birthday became important. We surprised him with a lunch complete with birthday cake and a present. Joe had become a part of life at the parish centre. It was Joe's twenty-sixth birthday. What a thrill it was to see the expression of joy on his face. Life was not easy for Joe, because an invalid pension didn't go far when you had to pay for your flat and buy food. Life was a struggle, so remembering and celebrating his birthday was very important.

Sadly, many people grow up without celebrating birthdays. One young lad staying with us at St Kilda had his thirteenth birthday with us. He didn't know what to do with his presents and what to do with the cake and the candles. There were lumps in our throats on that night over a simple thing like a birthday party.

Cup Day Australian people love to have a little wager on the Melbourne Cup. Even if they never have a bet for the rest of the year, on this day it's bordering on 'religion'. Over the years, in both Yarraville and St Kilda parishes, Cup Day has brought with it heaps of fun.

We conducted a Melbourne Cup Sweep in Yarraville in a novel way. When the nominations came out in July, about four months before the famous '1st Tuesday in November', we ran our sweep. Approximately 450–500 horses were nominated and for $1.00 you were at least guaranteed to get a horse! Of course only twenty-four of those nominations would eventually make it to the barrier. It was advertised as a 'fun sweep' with all of the entry money being given away in prizes. For the winner, it was a big prize.

On Cup Day at St Kilda we have a day in our hall for people of our area. There are television screens for people to watch the races; there is afternoon tea served virtually non-stop for a couple of hours; there is the chance to enter a sweep and above all, there is the chance to have a little wager on the Cup! It's all in good fun.

Many of the people who attend the Cup Day social are on invalid pension or other benefits. There is always a supply of coins on hand so people can have a little 'flutter' on the Cup. I can vouch for the honesty of the system because I'm the bookmaker.

Christmas dinner One of the Melbourne parishes has made a tremendous commitment to the people who frequent Sacred Heart Mission. East Ringwood is almost an hour's drive from St Kilda, but for ten years people from there have been rostered to assist with the daily hall meal on virtually every Monday. It has been a wonderful commitment from generous people of a generous parish.

This generosity comes to a climax with the provision of Christmas dinner with all the trimmings, all donated by the East Ringwood parishioners. Even the Mission team are invited to sit back and relax on this day and enjoy the hospitality. There is an 'invasion' of volunteers from East Ringwood. Over 400 people sit down to Christmas dinner during a two-hour period, and each person receives a Christmas present. While people are enjoying the meal, some of the volunteers sing Christmas Carols. It's a great day.

The dinner is provided on Christmas eve. On the next day we manage to have enough food from the leftovers to provide Christmas lunch, usually for 200 people who have nowhere to go on this day.

I'm sure that Jesus had a good time and wants us to enjoy life to the full. When people ask me how am I coping at St Kilda, I often reply with that silly phrase, 'I'm still happy in the circus!' And I am!

PART 4

Stories about living and loving

The stories which follow are a collection of episodes in my life in the various parishes. The names of people have been changed, although I am sure that many of the people would not mind their stories being made public.

There are stories of sadness which are an inevitable result of loving; there are stories which give hope through people's acceptance of each other; there are light-hearted stories which remind us of joy.

Some aspects of life place people on the fringe of society. Prostitution, drug addiction, psychiatric illness and alcoholism can all be 'fringe areas' of our society. To love people requires us to be non-judging, totally accepting and reaching out.

It was G. K. Chesterton who once said that 'loving means to love that which is unlovable—or it is no virtue at all'. I would like to believe that there is no such person as an 'unlovable person'. Such a statement becomes a challenge for the Christian.

Saying 'I love you'

David Rogers originally came from West Australia where he had university degrees and a responsible position. After marriage breakdowns, he had drifted into alcoholism and found himself in St Kilda. Although a chronic alcoholic, David never lost that level of respect and courtesy which must have been part and parcel of his earlier life before St Kilda. He was one of my 'specials'. At one stage David went away to an alcohol rehabilitation centre for several months and did extraordinarily well. But it didn't last.

David's general health was deteriorating. We used to talk about this, and he had a somewhat fatalistic approach to his health. He knew just how sick he was, but felt it was too late to make any dramatic change to his life. His health was so bad towards the end that the doctor wanted him to go to the hospital, but he refused. She rang me to see if I could manage to convince him. In his small room I discussed all this with him. He asked me why I kept at him and would not leave him be. 'Why won't you give up on me?' was his question. I remember looking him in the eye and saying, 'David, I guess it's because I love you.' He looked me in the eye and said, 'I know that, and I love you too'. We hugged each other. It's moments like this which happen when you work with people like David.

David went to the hospital and improved enough to come home, but then he deteriorated again very quickly. He collapsed and died in his room shortly afterwards. We arranged a funeral for David. A few people gathered in our church for the occasion. As I was talking about David, recalling special moments with him, I began to recall this moment. But I had to stop as I couldn't continue to speak. My eyes filled with tears at the remembrance of that moment. I had to say, 'Let's have a moment to pray for David', then I knelt down at the rails.

At the funeral Mass or service of our 'loners', the people who die without family, we always invite parishioners to join with the team and people around the Mission in this time of prayer. We are one family. The challenge is to build such a community that people are not forgotten and in particular, are cared for in sickness.

Getting a bit too close for comfort

'Mel' was a chronic alcoholic who died at the young age of thirty-two. He was known at the Mission as a man who could be very aggressive at times, but one who could be reached with persistence. That's one thing you need in great supply with such people. For a long time Mel lived in some outhouse rooms behind a condemned rooming house called 'Seaside Lodge', more commonly known to the locals as 'suicide lodge', because of the appalling conditions.

He moved to another rooming house when finally evicted from Seaside Lodge. This place was about one degree worse or one degree better, it was hard to tell! Some of the Mission team would visit the fellows in these places, just to keep an eye on how they were getting along. I was asked to go along and see Mel because he was very sick. I walked into one of the worst living situations possible, and there was Mel in a bad way. It was a Friday night. He was unconscious when I arrived and struggling to breathe. Cathy and I decided that he would have to go to hospital, so an ambulance was called. But Mel came around by the time the ambulance arrived. There was no way that he would go to the hospital. The ambulance left without Mel.

We yarned for awhile, and Mel said that all he wanted to do was watch the tennis on television which was coming from Wimbledon. He knew who would be playing, and he knew all the results from the previous day's tennis. We had a talk about his health, and he promised us that he would go to the hospital the next afternoon. If we came at 1 p.m., then he would go in the ambulance. As we walked home, I remarked to Cath that he would go because he had promised us, and he would keep his word to us. I saw this as a sign of the relationship of trust which we had developed by always 'hanging in' with Mel.

Next day, we arrived at the appointed time. Sure enough, he was prepared to go to the hospital. We rang the ambulance and saw him on his way, after which we stayed for a while to clear out his possessions. We didn't take much, just the important papers, his electrical goods and a few souvenirs and mementos. We reached the hospital to be greeted by the news that Mel was in a bath being deloused. The nursing staff said that they had never seen anybody with such lice infection. They asked whether we had been close to Mel in his room. 'Not too close' I replied. 'I had simply held him in my arms for about an hour waiting for the ambulance!' When we returned home, we had to go to the chemist to get some shampoo to rid ourselves of the lice.

Mel was critically ill and was admitted to hospital. We went through his letters and found some interesting items. One was a referral letter from a doctor to a specialist which was opened but never acted upon. The letter stated that unless Mel received immediate help, he would not live for very long. Mel knew how sick he was but had chosen not to take the necessary action. We also found a few letters from one person. These were all tied together. I read the letters and found a reference which indicated that this person was his sister. The letters indicated that he was loved by his sister. I found her phone number in Canberra and rang to inform her that Mel was dying. She in turn gave me his mother's number in Melbourne. She was also contacted. Mel's family renewed the contact which he had broken, and they attended the hospital regularly. This was appreciated by Mel and brought him peace and comfort.

The wedding family

At Yarraville parish, one of the delightful undertakings had been the involvement of our parish with the migrant hostel at Maribyrnong. This was the receiving place for refugees from southeast Asia. Pat Johnson, later to work with me in St Kilda, was the welfare officer at the hostel and had a young woman from Laos named Ha Phonerany as her assistant.

It was great for Ha when her fiancee, Phasouk, arrived in Australia. They had been separated through refugee camps in southeast Asia, and it took some time for Phasouk and Ha to find each other. Plans were now underway for their wedding celebration. They approached me to see if I could marry them. Finding a way that made this possible, the wedding was arranged for St Augustine's Church in Yarraville. As they had no direct family in Australia, the centre pages of the weekly parish newsletter were in the form of a wedding invitation.

The parishioners of St Augustine's Church were invited to the wedding of Ha Phonerany and Phasouk Vichidvongsa. No RSVP was necessary. The wedding itself, although Christian in its outline, included some of the Laotian cultural ceremony. Quite a group of people from the parish arrived, complete with wedding presents for the couple.

Afterwards we adjourned to the parish house, where I was living, for the wedding reception. The manager of the hostel presented the bride at the wedding and also made the speech at the reception. Pat Johnson had baked a wedding cake. We had a full reception at the house.

When it was Phasouk's time to respond, he made a beautiful speech. He referred to their families in Laos not knowing how they were. He indicated how the people gathered for the wedding were their new family. Phasouk went on in this vein for some time and there were few dry eyes in the room at that time. It was a most beautiful moment, and a moment of love for all those present.

An introduction to a sad world

One of the first people to become part of our open house was Peter, whom we later came to know as Colin Puckeridge. He was known to us as 'Shades' and was a lovely young man who became part of our home, sitting at the kitchen table, chatting away, welcoming other people to the table. It was hard to reconcile this picture with that of a young man with an addiction who was eventually to overdose.

His name was Peter Koustevikis, but he was commonly known among his friends as 'Shades'. We were his friends, so he was Shades to us too. His addiction to drugs had led to him being on crutches because of a leg injury.

We received word that Shades had been found dead from an overdose in his room and had been removed to the city mortuary. I still feel the questions which raced through my mind as I went to clear the room after his death. Aware of a wasted young life, wondering about his family and where they may be. People like Colin force you to ask lots of questions about life and lead you to a better understanding of human frailty. Kate Wilson and I did the formal identification of the body. Then came the job of waiting to find out whether there were any relatives. Word eventually came that his real name was Colin Puckeridge and contact was made with his mother, Betty, in Sydney.

We contacted a priest in Sydney to visit Betty and find out her circumstances. She was already paying for the funeral of an elder brother of Colin who had also died from a drug overdose. Betty was a battler and agreed to let us share the cost of burying her son and also to accept an airfare to Melbourne to stay with us for a few days.

Just two days before Betty was due to arrive for the funeral, the police suspected that this was not Colin Puckeridge at all, but some other person who had been using Colin's name. The priest in Sydney visited Betty and, on some pretext, got a recent photo of her son before the Friday funeral. We met the Ansett plane at midnight on Thursday night to collect a special package containing the photograph of Betty's son. Thankfully, and I think that is the right word, the photo did verify that the young man who had died was Colin.

After the funeral the next day, Betty stayed at the Mission for a few days and took part in everything happening around the place. She helped prepare meals at lunch, provided cups of tea for visitors and paddled around the kitchen in her bare feet. She was right at home. She drew strength in her sadness from staying with us at the Mission. That contact with Betty has continued over the years and reminds us that care of people beyond death is essential.

My first experience

'Mary' was the first woman I met who was involved in prostitution. Shortly after my arrival in St Kilda she came to the presbytery. She had been released from prison a few days earlier. She was broke and back on the street, but not really from choice. From that day, she held a special place in my life. She taught me so much about a life in prostitution. Through Mary, I learned to ignore what people may be thinking. The first time I sat on a fence on Grey Street and talked with her, I began to be aware of what people might be thinking of me.

I remember one rather amusing incident with Mary. We were always trying to make time for a cuppa and a chat. One morning I asked her to come in to the Mission. She said she couldn't because she had to work, to which I replied, 'Well, you've got to have a morning tea break, don't you?' I think that I even surprised myself with the offer.

Finding a home

Barry Stirling had been around St Kilda for some time and was a regular around the Mission. One of our workers, Margaret Hayes, worked closely with Barry and was caring for him when he was diagnosed as having terminal cancer. For months, his life was to be in and out of hospital for treatment. He needed a secure, supportive home base. Barry moved into one of our houses and contact was made with some of his family. His sickness lasted for a long time, with a slow deterioration of his health. At no stage did he become despairing. He always remained peaceful and appreciative of the care shown to him whether by the hospital, the nurses or people from our Mission, especially Margaret. His sisters became frequent visitors and cared for him also. He felt secure and supported.

Through care and interest over a long period of time, Barry was able to feel part of a 'family' when he became sick. In that family he found support and the strength to live out his sickness peacefully. He was at home. Eventually he was admitted to hospital and died peacefully. Barry was also buried at Emerald Cemetery as this was his wish.

What a voice

'Troy' was one of the first people I met in St Kilda. He was one of those local characters with his own particular way. He had his own particular voice which could be heard from a great distance. He could be the most annoying person at times, especially in the church. He would plant himself in the front row and give a running commentary on my sermon and on the Mass. Sometimes, he would go past the limit, whatever the limit may be, and action would be required. On one particular occasion, he started his 'commentary' in a voice that could be heard everywhere in the church. This would be tolerable, but I was distributing Communion, and he was in the front seat a few feet away. I can't write in this book my message to Troy on this occasion, but I stopped what I was doing and went over to give him a very direct message. I hope the Lord understood what I was saying and doing, Troy certainly did. He shut up which was a blessing for everyone.

Troy had that way of knowing just how far he could go, but sometimes he went one step too far and then decisive action was required, such as carting him out of the church. The same procedure was also required now and again out in the hall meal room. But Troy would always bounce back again. I recall another moment when he was told that one of the men had died. He simply said, 'I must say a prayer for him'. Troy closed his eyes and said his prayer then and there. I haven't seen Troy for awhile, but I can still hear his voice loud and clear in my memory.

A place for Don

Call this man 'Don'. He is in his late 70s and not a Catholic. However, he has attended Mass regularly for his wife since her death many years ago. He now feels the need for confession. We had a long chat, and then I invited him to spend a little time alone in the Yarraville chapel. I prepared a few things for his reception into full Communion with the Church. Thelma, Sister Bernadette and I began to pray with and for Don. In that little chapel Don was received into the Church and given the forgiveness he was seeking. Then he was anointed with the sacred oil in the sacrament of the sick. We left Don in the quiet of the chapel for some time. The following Sunday, Don received the Eucharist for the first time. He became a regular member of our congregation. Don found peace in his new faith which he expressed with other people in our parish family. A quick conversion? Not really, what happened was an endorsement of his deep faith.

A lesson for life

In Sandringham parish, one of my duties was to attend the Cheltenham cemetery. I would meet the funeral on arrival and conduct the prayers at the graveside. It was here that I carried out my first funeral for a person with no-one in attendance and his name was Edwin Lewis.

At the funeral of Edwin Lewis, in attendance were me, the undertakers and the gravedigger. I mentioned this to the congregation at Sandringham on the following Sunday and invited them to pray for Edwin because there was no one else in the world to pray for him. During the following week, several families came to have a special Mass offered for him and pray for him as a family. This was a lovely response.

A year later, Kath Maher approached me and asked me for an anniversary Mass for Edwin Lewis. I had to ask Kath who

Edwin Lewis was. When she told me, I thanked her. I knew that I would never forget Edwin Lewis again. She had remembered him in her prayers and was having Mass offered on the anniversary of his death. This example of one person taking to themselves the life and death of another person was inspiring to me.

A new world for me

One Sunday afternoon, shortly after my arrival in St Kilda, a fellow knocked at the back door. This made me a bit doubtful because there is a big front door with a 'welcome' mat and a bell. Anyway, I met this fellow, a stranger I came to know as 'William'. He needed the priest to come to his mate who was seriously ill. I happened to be having about a dozen people for dinner, and they were just arriving. I excused myself and assured them that I would be back within fifteen or twenty minutes because it was almost certainly nothing serious.

When I arrived at the flat, I discovered 'Ralph' who was dying from the effects of alcoholism. Ralph was on a stretcher in the flat. On the bed was Wolfgang, the official tenant of the flat. He looked even worse than Ralph! There was a crowd in the one-room flat looking after Ralph who was adamant that he was not going to the hospital. Eventually I went back to have dinner with my guests! I returned again later with Cathy Stewart. We decided to care for Ralph at home to the best of our ability and that of his friends.

The next couple of weeks were a privilege for all of us, the carers and the cared for. After a few days Wolfgang was moved out to a place where he could receive some care. He improved immensely and is still in one of our houses. The next day, Bert, another fellow residing in this flat, suggested that he also might go off to the same place if I thought it was a good idea. Before he could change his mind, Bert was out of the flat and on his way to my car with not even the chance to put his shoes and socks on. He also went on to recover. John, another person also suffering from alcoholism, took up residence in Wolfgang's bed and kept watch over Ralph.

This level of care in this flat was demanding because Ralph had become completely dependent upon us. After a couple of weeks, Ralph had reached the stage where even helping him into the shower was simply too much for him. He was taken to the hospital where he died the next day. From the confidence these people had in us and from our availability, we entered into a relationship with William, Wolfgang, Bert, John, Camelia and others which has remained until this day.

Getting involved

The invitation to be involved with the emergency house of the Catholic Family Welfare Bureau came as a response to a talk to the parish council. Several parishes were invited by the bureau to find volunteers for this group, but Yarraville was the only parish to respond. This group of six or seven ladies stayed together for ten years. They raised money through cake stalls and other events. They cleaned the houses and supported the women in the emergency housing programme in little ways. In fact they did anything that was needed. I do recall that they got away to a great start with the first house. The bureau found the appropriate house to begin this programme. Then the ladies spent days cleaning it thoroughly, furnishing it and getting ready for the big day. The first family were ready to move in. The ladies went around to the house and gave it the final cleaning-up. On that very first night, the woman of the house decided to light a fire to keep warm, but preferred the middle of the floor rather than the fireplace! Disaster! It was a case of one day cleaning the place to get ready, and the next day cleaning up after the fire brigade had done their job in putting out the fire. What a great start! But this little group persevered. They formed themselves into a monthly prayer group as well. It was a case of a group of ladies integrating their faith and their care for others.

A big night for us

Our first attempt at managing a rooming-house got away to a fiery start! We took over a house at a cheap rental because it was in poor condition. There were seven rooms in the main house with four bungalows out the back. Our first move was to have a barbecue. We provided the food and the works, the residents provided the beer and other assorted drinks. It was a good fun gathering, and we got to know each other. Some of the men had not met each other, although some had lived there for a long time. There was also one woman in this group of residents.

After just seven months, there came an early morning phone call. The house was on fire. Cath and I headed off immediately and discovered how lucky everyone had been. One of the men, Les, usually the one who slept the heaviest, had woken up to the sound of possums in the roof. But it wasn't possums, it was fire. He yelled out to the people in the house and then raced out to the bungalows. By that time, he could not get back into the house, the old weatherboard house was ablaze.

After things settled down, it was back to the presbytery in the Mission bus. At 4 a.m., we were sitting in the lounge room drinking coffee and talking. There was fear mixed with relief, loss mixed with laughter. What impressed me was the sense of 'belonging' that existed among this group of people after such a short time in our rooming-house.

Grassroots Christianity

'Donna' was one of those people who come into your life and make an indelible impression. Donna had been around Sacred Heart Mission for some time and had a background of psychiatric illness. She came to live in one of our houses, and so we came to know her very well. Donna decided that she wanted to become a Catholic. She was about sixty and had experienced a lot of hurt, suffering and struggle in her life. I felt that Donna did not need much instruction in the sense of formal teaching. She mainly wanted a sense of belonging to a community of people who cared for her and for whom she cared. Becoming a Catholic was a serious matter for Donna, so I suggested to Sister Angela that it should take at least six weeks for Donna to become instructed. All that was needed was a very basic understanding of Jesus. Did Donna believe in God and love Jesus, understand that Jesus was present in the Eucharist, say her prayers and go to Mass, try to be good and helpful to people, and so forth. Eventually the big day arrived and Donna was received into the Catholic Church in St Kilda.

About six months later Donna came to inform me that she wished to be married. She had met Arthur, a Catholic who had never been married. Would it be all right to get married at Sacred Heart Church. Unfortunately, this was to be Donna's third marriage. This was a problem. I explained to her that I could not marry her in the Catholic Church so she felt that she would ask Reverend Peter at the Presbyterian church to marry her. Things were going smoothly now. Then she asked, in a way that implied the answer would be 'no', 'This won't make any difference to me being a Catholic and coming to Communion will it?' How else could I answer!

I was to find out later on from Reverend Peter just what a grassroots understanding of church Donna had. Since her reception into the Catholic Church, Donna had been a regular every Sunday, attending Mass and receiving Communion. However, as she put it to me, because Reverend Peter had been so good to her and not wanting to hurt his feelings, she had also been going to the Presbyterian church on a Sunday evening and receiving Communion there too.

I learned from Donna that for the wedding she had arranged a table at a local hotel for four people—her and Arthur and their two witnesses. I felt we could do better than this. So I asked Wendy Lanyon who had been working closely with Donna, to arrange an invitation list for the wedding. The reception was to take place in the dining room at the presbytery, and formal invitations were sent out to about twenty people. Women from the Ashburton parish came along to provide the meal and to serve the dinner for the wedding breakfast. One of the women from Ashburton also made the wedding cake. The group of guests, mainly from Sacred Heart Mission, all headed off to the Presbyterian church for the wedding; then we all adjourned to the Catholic presbytery for the reception What a great day it turned out to be.

As a wedding present from the Mission we presented Donna and Arthur with a return rail ticket to Warrnambool, a fair distance away in the country, along with one week's accommodation at a motel. We had already contacted the owners of the motel to look after this elderly couple during their stay. All in all it was a happy experience. Entering into a life of shared love with Donna had taken us on a journey which stepped beyond the 'rules' of the Church. However with her own special grassroots understanding of God and church, we were left without any choices. She understood in her own special way.

Donna died a couple of years later and we all attended the funeral. As Vanier stated, we had entered into life with Donna which would draw us into bonds of love to which we would be tied for life.

A simple gift

There was a Lebanese family living in the small street which ran from the church to the house in which I was living at

Yarraville. I would traverse that street many times in the course of a week and walk past this particular house. The young Lebanese men living there had just brought their parents out from Lebanon. The parents didn't speak one word of English. We were informed that when they came, my cousin Thelma and I would be invited to have a cup of coffee with their parents. We did this and sat in the room with the elderly couple, neither of whom spoke English. As we spoke no Lebanese, it was simply a question of nodding to each other over a cup of very strong coffee. We had been made welcome and a communication had begun.

The old man was often in the front garden with his flowers and vegetables. I would stop and chat with him as best I could and teach him a few English words. This particular day, his first two flowers were out and I gestured to them and said 'flower, beautiful'. He eventually understood what I meant and smiled and said 'beautiful' and broke off the flower to give to me. I was embarrassed by this. I gestured to our house and said 'Thelma', meaning that I would give this flower to her. He understood immediately, smiled and said 'Thelma' and broke off the other flower! Now I was even more embarrassed. So I headed off with his first two flowers.

A chain of circumstances

I was called to the home of one of our parishioners, Pat Fanning, who had been found dead. Pat was a single lady who had retired from work after many years and lived alone in her flat in St Kilda. She was a quiet lady, very friendly, a devout Catholic and a nice lady around the church. One of your ordinary parishioners— always there.

Pat had collapsed at home and, by the apparent circumstances, had died immediately. It was not until quite a few days later that something was known to be wrong and, sad but true, it was because of the unpleasant stench from the flat. The police had been called. I was notified and went to pray over the body of Pat. There is no need for me to describe the situation which was most unpleasant. I was able to carry out the identification for the police and later on officially identify her. This saved her relatives a most unpleasant task.

Pat's elderly sister, an invalid, arrived by taxi with her invalid husband, and I spent time with them outside in the taxi. I was able to dissuade them from going into the flat. I assured them that Pat had not suffered. These are all moments that stay with you.

The same is true of the death of Doris Wilson, another older woman living alone in St Kilda, retired from her work, living in a flat, a regular at church and so on. By a chain of circumstances, over the Christmas vacation period, the people who usually brought her to Mass presumed she was away with relatives. Again, it was only after a week or two that she was found dead in the flat. She had also died without suffering. The fact still remains that she died alone and remained alone for some time before she was found.

This fact of people dying alone and not being found for some time is another one of those challenges to our society. We must be aware of each other and responsible for each other as a local community. In Glenhuntly parish, an elderly man had collapsed and fallen against the piano. His elderly sister went into a state of shock and walked aimlessly around the house. More than a week later the situation was discovered. By this time the man was badly ulcerated where he had fallen against the piano and was close to death. He died a couple of days later. The sister could not be 'reached' in conversation. After the event, some people remarked that he hadn't been in the garden as he usually was. It's important that we see not only what is before us but what is not before us.

The happy drunk

Another character was 'Jack'. He was one who used to be on the beach, sleeping out, always bright and happy. Amazingly, the drunker he would get, the better would be his somersaults down the hill! He was always courteous to us at the Mission.

I was called by the owner of a rooming house to get Jack out of a room occupied by his drinking companion. Jack was in a bad way, but he was as happy as ever, drinking orange juice and methylated spirits. I took with me one of the Jesuit students, who was spending some of his novitiate with us. On this visit Jack was his usual welcoming, smiling, respectful self. I told Jack that he would have to leave the room. A few things were sorted out and I told Jack that we would also have to tip out his 'mixture' because it was bad for him. So Jack moved out of the room and everyone settled down again.

The big news came about a week later. Jack had been admitted to a detox centre and was doing well. From the clinic he moved out to Corpus Christi Community at Greenvale, a place for men to make a home for themselves. He stayed there for four years and then came back to St Kilda to one of our group houses. This wasn't the right set-up for Jack. After awhile he moved to his own flat, and he is still there. Jack has been totally sober for eight years. He is able to walk into the pubs and help out the fellows who are broke. Jack is the 'lemon squash king'.

A real-life St Veronica

It was Saturday night at St Kilda and I was heading across for the evening Mass. I was greeted by Kevin McCarthy, one of the regular helpers at the church, with the news that 'We've got some trouble tonight Father'. I asked what the trouble was. Kevin informed me that there was a woman in the church who was drunk and he couldn't move her. I looked down the long aisle of the church and saw the woman sitting in front of the main altar in a yoga position which, as I said to Kevin, could mean that she was saying her prayers.

As I walked up the aisle and got closer to the lady, I was very aware that she was in a bad way. Her general appearance was very dirty and she certainly smelled. I knelt down alongside of her and tried to persuade her to sit up so that I could talk to her. No response. I asked her to lift her head so that I could see who she was. No response. I was getting nowhere.

In the front row of the church Kath Hamilton was saying her prayers. Kath was a refined elderly lady who always came early to the church. She rose from her seat and came towards the lady and knelt down. This lovely lady spoke to the dishevelled woman saying 'lift up your head dear, Father Ernie cannot help you unless you do'. The woman lifted up her face straight away. And what a mess she was. Her hair was dirty and matted, her eyes were wet. She had been crying. Her nose was running, and her mouth had been dribbling; she looked quite pathetic. She was a young woman in her late twenties. Kath's response was simply, 'Oh, my dear, look what a mess you've made of yourself. Here, let me tidy you up'. Kath took a lovely handkerchief from her handbag and proceeded to wipe the young woman's face, nose and mouth, and then said, 'Now that's better. You look much better. Now sit up in the front seat where Father can talk to you'. And the lady did just that. She got up, sat in the seat and we proceeded to have a talk.

Here was the legend of St Veronica wiping the face of Jesus in a modern day context. In a simple and loving way Kath had to go beyond those things that can put one off from helping another person. There was the smell, the appearance, the dirt and the alcoholism. Through speaking to the woman and through wiping her face, Kath had gone past the facade to reach the person.

Breaking my own rules

'Ian' was an older man who had been part of the drug life for a long time. He came through the mission with his girlfriend 'Ruth' looking for help to sort out their lives. They both went off to centres for help and, to the best of my knowledge, are still doing well. Ruth has found support through her regular attendance at Narcotics Anonymous (NA) meetings and has settled down with her daughter making a new life. For awhile, they lived in our women's house. It's a great feeling for us to see her doing well.

Ian was a different story. After being at a rehabilitation centre for a spell, he came out and returned to St Kilda feeling great. But he started struggling and began to work in the hall assisting with the preparation of the meals. This went well, but then he came to see me one day after the lunch meal. He was in a mess. He was sweating, shaking and aching. He asked me for money for a 'fix' just to get him through the moment. I went outside to talk with Cathy and we talked and worried for awhile. I would never have thought it possible, but I did give him the money for heroin. It turned my stomach upside down in the process. At that time I was involved in a drug assistance centre. I told my friend Peter Bucci what I had done. He couldn't believe it, nor could I for that matter. And then I added, 'Peter, I did it twice!' That was one of my most horrible experiences.

Shortly after this, with a bit of help, Ian went away to Darwin to a centre for drug addicted people. The centre is thousands of miles from Melbourne and St Kilda. That was it. No more word from Ian. Then, after three years, he appeared back at the Mission looking fantastic—healthy, strong, well groomed and confident. I can't tell you in words how good it was to see him again.

Hopelessness?

On Easter Night in 1989 I was having an early night after the
Vigil ceremonies. I had forgotten to go to a twenty-first
birthday party. This turned out to be a 'happy fault'. I awoke
about 11 p.m. to the doorbell, but there was no-one at the
door. I paddled outside barefoot to see if I could find the
person. There was 'Virginia' walking down the sideway. She
came in and wanted a chat and then wanted to go to the toilet.
Now Virginia had been in a rehabilitation centre, so I rang
Cathy Stewart to see what was happening with her. I learned
she had been discharged a few days earlier but was not doing
so well.

I felt that Virginia was using drugs in the toilet, so I kept up
a constant chatter with her. Suddenly she collapsed in the
toilet, but I couldn't open the door properly, only enough to
see that she had overdosed badly. I rang Cathy, Sister Patricia
at the convent and also the ambulance. From then it was
hectic, but the short version is that the ambulance men kept
her alive when she stopped breathing at one point on the way
to the hospital.

Next morning, on my way to 8 a.m. Mass, I couldn't
believe my eyes. There was Virginia on the street. I said to
her, 'What the hell are you doing here, Virginia. You died last
night!' She replied that she had nowhere else to go, and this
was true. A few days later Virginia headed off to a detox and
rehabilitation centre. Six months later I could point to Virginia
as one who had made it home.

The sad postscript to the story of Virginia is that she died
of an overdose in Sydney at the end of 1989. She had stayed
in a programme for eight months. The word was that this was
her first use of heroin after so long. But the love we
experienced with Virginia remains. Failure? Not really,
because there was love. Her death came as an end to a life
struggle.

What is success

The week after Virginia overdosed in the presbytery, there was a banging on the side door of the church as I began Mass on Saturday night. I threw my keys to someone and continued, but the keys didn't come back. That kept me guessing through Mass. After Mass, I found the reason was that a girl named Marie had been found overdosed alongside the church. Cath Stewart was called and now Marie was in the parlour coming out of it.

A couple of hours later we felt that, apart from the overdose, something was not right. So Marie was taken to hospital and admitted. We were told that she may have died from internal bleeding without hospital care.

A few weeks later Marie overdosed again and was clinically dead on arrival at the hospital. She was revived but was brain damaged and remained in a coma for several weeks. She now lies in a bean bag in a country hospital unaware of people and the world around her.

I would ask people, 'Which one is success?' We would maintain that with both Virginia and Marie, there was success. Both were loved and knew that they were loved, and both in their own way loved in return. This is the measure of success in so much of the work of the Mission with people 'on the fringe'.

With Marie, we hold a precious memory. While in the hospital, she had her twenty-fifth birthday. She was in a single room, but Cath and I decided that we would celebrate her birthday. We were there virtually every day, talking to her, hoping that she may be hearing us or recognising us, but to no apparent avail. The night before, we decorated her room with streamers and balloons to make things bright, and then came her birthday.

Cath went into the room while I spoke with the sisters. When I walked in, I started whistling 'Happy Birthday'.

Immediately Marie turned to me and smiled. That simple little tune seems to go on forever when your stomach is turning over, there is a lump in your throat and tears welling in your eyes. There was this brief time of recognition. And yes I knew that we loved each other.

Burial-continuing the love

In St Kilda people dying alone is not an uncommon event. Care in this regard has become a special form of our ministry. After about eighteen months in St Kilda, a young man we had come to know was found dead in his room. Those of us at the Mission felt that we would like to bury him. However, we had very little money and decided that we had better keep our money to care for those who were alive. After all, as long as we prayed for Greg and attended the graveside, it didn't really matter that he was to be buried in an unmarked pauper grave. That's what we thought in 1983. Over the years, this attitude changed. We came to see that care for a person in death is really a continuation of the care we have shown in the person's life.

The way in which we enter into the life of a person with love and care, means that we take on a commitment to follow that relationship through to the grave. This is true not only from our point of view, but from the point of view of quite a few people around the Mission. They have come to know and expect that the Mission will take care of them when they die. For us it has become an expression of our love for them.

All of us, whether priest or lay person, have our own pet themes. One of mine is, 'We fail when someone dies alone'.

Now obviously, in a city parish, there will be many people who, for one reason or another, withdraw from society and community life. Some of these people will die alone. The challenge to the church as a community of Christians is to prevent this happening to the best of its ability.

My own school mate

In 1970, there was a school reunion of the boys of '51 at my sister's home. With Michael Keogh, I went to see one of our '51 school mates, Peter Maguire, who was in a bad way with an alcohol problem. We received a wary welcome from Peter's wife Valerie because she thought that we were detectives! Anyway, Peter was a mess. But he said that he would get to the reunion, didn't need a lift and wouldn't drink at the party. A big statement given the state he was in.

Peter was the first to arrive at the party, and all day he kept away from the grog. He was very sick, far worse than we first thought. I drove Peter home from the reunion with the boot of my car holding the left-over bottles of beer. Peter wanted a drink, but he also said that he wanted to try and stay 'straight'. The next day he joined me on an altar boys' picnic, which wouldn't be the ideal place for someone trying to go straight. This was the first of many days with me.

Over the next couple of years, Peter and I spent a lot of time together. We had some great happy times with his family and my family. We had the terrible moments as well. Peter was too broken physically and mentally to make a recovery, and his death truly was an end to the struggle. He died in 1972 from the effects of alcoholism.

Peter made many friends with the members of the football team which I was coaching in Sandringham at the time. He came to the games and even to training nights. After his death, the players got together and had 'working bees' at his house to assist his wife and children. The walls of the house were stripped and repainted and the spouting and downpipes replaced. Through it all there was evidence of the respect which people had for Peter. This respect gave Peter a chance to have some peace and happiness during the last two years of his life.

A good start to married life

On one occasion, we celebrated a wedding in the Chapel of the St Kilda Mission House because there were only the four people involved—the bride and groom and the two witnesses. Carmel, the bride, was a volunteer at the mission with the hall meal. Our house cat Ebony disgraced himself on the day of the wedding in the chapel by leaving an unwanted deposit there. The groom discovered this while waiting for me to arrive with the papers, so he scored the good job of removing the offending article! A good start to married life, I suppose.

To always be there

'Ray' was one of the early people to become part of the mission. He had a heavy addiction to 'speed' over a long period. He was staying in an old run-down house which we rented for a couple of years. The Jesuit students stayed there at the end of 1982 as part of their pastoral experience with us. They gained a lot of experience in that house because the walls were thin. Ray and his girlfriend of the time gave them a few sleepless nights as they raged on while the students were supposed to be asleep. Ray was one who ran 'hot and cold' with this addiction, sometimes seeming to move ahead and at other times going backwards. He would be classed as a bit of a 'con' with us at the mission. But he was special. He was around our mission on and off for a long time. I developed a 'soft spot' for Ray.

At one stage we arranged for Ray to stay at a country presbytery in Nagambie. The parish priest, Father Frank Marriott, gave a welcome and hospitality to Ray, with the opportunity to get away from the city for a new start. This wasn't a roaring success, but it was another important step which would form a part of his eventual freedom from drugs. He then moved into a relationship with a 'straight' lady with a couple of children. They had a house in the country, and things were going along smoothly. But this wasn't to last either. About this time, my old car was on its last days, and I purchased another car. I gave the old car to Ray to work on and use for himself. When I visited him one day in the country, he told me that the car needed a fair amount of work and would cost too much, but he felt that he could get a sum of money by selling it for parts. I told Ray that I had given him the car, and he could have whatever he could get for it.

End of story? Not quite. We lost touch with him. Ray made contact with us several years later and he looked fantastic. What a great thrill. He was living in a country town with a good lady whom he hoped to marry one day. He was holding down a regular job, had made new friends and was clean of drugs for many years. And the old car? It was with the money from the car that he had moved to this new town to make a completely new start.

Ray taught me much about drug addiction. The need for patience and waiting, the place for forgiveness and understanding, the times for strength and firmness and saying 'No'. But above all, to always be there is the key. Ray may have 'conned' us sometimes, but in all of this, he knew and we knew that we cared for each other. That's what counts in the end.

The ordinary things of life

One day Cathy Stewart asked one of the women in our Women's House to pop on the kettle and make a cup of tea. Soon she realised that nothing had happened and turned to see what was wrong. 'How do you put the kettle on?' was the question and the problem. Such a simple thing! Another time Cathy asked one woman to soak the label off a coffee jar. 'Use really hot water' was the direction given. When Cath came out to the kitchen, she found the bottle on the bench full of very hot water. It would take a long while to soak off the label from inside. Funny? Not really! Very sad.

Christmas time brought forth a question which completely stunned Cath. 'What do people do on Christmas Day?' This woman, as an adult, could not remember a Christmas Day spent in a 'family' situation. A question like this goes straight to your middle. It is upsetting, but it shows the importance of the 'little things' of living.

A refugee baby

At Yarraville, tragedy gave us the chance to reach out to care for refugees. Yia Thaia was a little baby of nine months and had been in Melbourne at the hostel just two weeks before he became very sick and died in the Children's Hospital. His parents were a young couple. Blong, the father, was only twenty-two, and Mao Lee, the mother, was twenty years old. They came from an area in the mountains of Laos. As refugees they had hoped to begin a new life of peace in our country. They had no family here and spoke no English. They had no money, and our parish had the privilege of helping them in this sad time.

Arrangements were made with the local undertaker. He was very generous in his charges because of the situation. The parish refugee committee then paid the minimal bill for the funeral costs. The Buddhist priest attended the funeral and carried out all the ceremonies. Some of us from the parish attended and stood with the people who had come together for the funeral. They were from the Hmong Association, the area of Laos where these two young parents were born. Afterwards all these people, few of whom could speak English, returned to the parish centre for afternoon tea.

Time for a hug

'Janet' was staying at the Women's House. I said to Cathy Stewart one day that Janet was busting for a cuddle from me, but the move would have to come from her. Well, one day I was standing in the front hallway talking to someone when she came through the door with Cathy. After a brief greeting, she stood alongside me while I kept on talking. After awhile, she put her arm around my back. A little later she moved around in front and faced me with both arms around me. I had my arms around her by this time. She snuggled in while I continued talking. Fortunately, she is short so I could talk over her head. Finally, we were hugging and rocking and still not a word between us. We all have a need for closeness and hugging and loving.

One day on the street, when Janet was not going so well, we had a bit of a cuddle. I was encouraging her to have another go at getting off the drugs. I told her that I loved her, and she replied that she loved me too. And it was and is true. There is a love between us which is special. Today she is still a bit of a mess.

An event of significance for Janet was the baptism of her two-year-old baby. Cathy had made the date for this on several occasions, but something always went wrong. Eventually, Janet felt that if the baby was to be baptised, so should she! There wasn't much point in catechumenate or heavy instruction, but something was needed. But, for one reason or another, this preparation didn't eventuate. The day was set, the foster parents arrived with the child and the godparents were there, but no Janet. The 12.30 p.m. time moved along, and I said to Cath that we would have to draw the line somewhere; 1.30 p.m. would be the latest time. At 1.25 p.m., I said, 'That's it, Cath'. Then I started putting things away. Wouldn't you believe it, Janet came through the door of the church in a flurry and all set to go.

Well, two baptisms took place. I am only the instrument of God's sacraments and sometimes God has to do a bit more work than us. This was one of those occasions. This was a most important and significant event. People like Janet, with their story of hurt, abuse and low self-esteem, need all the signs of love and care that are possible. The baptism, with all its hassles and shortcomings, was certainly that.

St Kilda's response to Ethiopia

One response at St Kilda is worth recalling. Ethiopia was at a peak of need. The newspapers and television showed how extreme the drought was. There were images of people dying of starvation. This happened on a Saturday, and I felt I needed to talk about it at the Saturday night Mass. My feeling was that we had to respond in some way. In the face of such an enormous tragedy, we feel insignificant. Money was not and is not the answer, but we still have to do this much at least. Without any prior notice, some people collected money after Mass. This was repeated on the Sunday. The following week, I announced that the special box at the back of the church should remain there until the crisis had abated. There will be no receipts for taxation. Simply put your money in the box. St Kilda is certainly not a wealthy parish and our annual collection at that time was around $28,000 or $550 per week. The box stayed in the church for a year, and our parish collected $14,000 which was an enormous response. It was a good example of people linking church and mission.

A cruel sickness

In the case of schizophrenia it is difficult to comprehend the level of confusion in people's minds. What we can do is grow in our understanding of the hurt which this sickness causes to the people. I was taking a man to the psychiatric hospital for admission. He was suffering from schizophrenia, and it had been this way for a long time. Things were not good at this particular moment, and he needed extra care. He said to me 'this is a cruel sickness Father'. A simple statement such as that, and the obvious struggle of the person at that moment, gave me another small insight into the struggle and the sickness. We need those moments.

'Mitch' suffered from schizophrenia. Sadly Mitch was found dead in a park near the church. He had hanged himself. So often we conclude that people who take their own lives don't know what they are doing because they are so depressed. In Mitch's case, depression would be seen as the cause. However, at age forty-one, if he looked back over the past twenty years he would see a life in which he had been in and out of the hospital, subject to constant medication, unable to maintain a stable relationship or have a girlfriend, unable to hold down a job, moving from place to place. It was not a very happy life. If he were to look twenty years into the future, he could probably anticipate more of the same. In a way he could well decide 'I have suffered enough'. Depression? Yes. Tiredness? Definitely. Perhaps this is a bit simplistic, and perhaps I'm forgetting about hope, but nevertheless it is a real picture for many people.

An unusual experience

'Cindy' has been one girl who has given us a fair share of headaches. It's a funny thing, but the ones who cause the most trouble are also the ones with whom you have a 'soft spot' even though you can't get too close or help them. There have been the violent times with Cindy, but there have been the other moments.

One moment I recall with a smile was the Sunday afternoon when I heard her screaming outside the Mission House door. It had been 'one of those days' with things not going too much to plan and the last thing I wanted was Cindy in full flight. Anyway, at the front door I found old Father Jack Curtain who was coming to see me and Cindy! She was waving a knife around and screaming and swearing. I asked her to come in and settle down, and I took her to the kitchen. I put Jack in the front room for a minute.

Cindy told me that she had been stabbed, so I said 'hold on and I'll be there in a minute'. After a moment with Jack, I returned to the kitchen. The fact was that Cindy had been stabbed in the backside, so what greeted me was this bare backside sticking up in the air. Cindy, bent over, asked me 'What's it look like, Father?' At these times, it's important how you answer!! Anyway, I said, 'It looks alright to me'. But she insisted, 'Does it need stitches? Is it still bleeding? Have a closer look?' I had to get her to go across to the sink and get cleaned up saying 'that will make you feel better Cindy'.

In the meantime, I had seen Father Jack, and he was on his way. Now the next job, once she was eventually dressed again, was to get the knife from her. But no way, she was going to find that guy and 'cut his thing off'. After a long time, she settled down and we talked about how lucky she was because the man had tried to seriously hurt her. Mission accomplished, but no, 'will you walk down the street with me because I am frightened'. That was fair enough, so we walked down the hill and this gave the chance for more serious talk about what had happened.

She then asked me for a loan of a dollar to buy some condoms. The next request I couldn't manage, 'Will you go and buy them for me at the adult shop across the road?' I asked a reason for this, 'Because I owe the fellow $1 already.' Well, after all this, I said, 'Cindy here's $2, $1 for your debt and $1 for the new condoms'. This may have been aiding and abetting, but it had been quite a day!

A loner

Elmer Raddich died alone in the gardens only 100 yards from our presbytery. Through our work at the Mission, we had known Elmer over a period of a few years. He was from Estonia. That was all we knew about his background. He had problems with alcoholism. He was a loner, and I guess much of this would be due to his background, whatever it was. Since his arrival in Australia from Europe, Elmer had been sleeping out in the parks. This day he was found dead in the morning. There is something added to the circumstances of death to be found alone in a garden.

Finding a new life

The Bethesda Centre at Mount Gambier has been a significant place for Sacred Heart Mission for quite a few years. It is conducted by the Lutheran church and, in those early years of contact, was managed by two men named Ross Goode and Maurie Thompson. These men seemed to have that 'special something' to reach the men who went there. Some men stay a short time but often return at a later date, while others have made their home in the town of Mount Gambier. At this time there are still six of our men who have never come back to Melbourne to live after having the chance to make a new life through Bethesda. 'Scott' is one of those six.

'Scott' was a young alcoholic man, a great fellow with a wonderful personality. He stayed with us at our home for awhile until a bed became available at Bethesda. In fact we celebrated his birthday while he was with us. We were having a double celebration at our house because both my father and Cath's father have the same birthday. Somewhere through the night we found out that it was also Scott's birthday, so he became part of a triple birthday celebration.

Scott did well at Bethesda. He came to grips with the problems behind the grog in his life. He also made his home in Mount Gambier. He became a youth counsellor and was involved in a myriad of programmes for young people. Scott found the Church through his involvement in an evangelical group. His conversion was an important factor in his rehabilitation and new life.

Responding to the immediate situation

One beautiful way for the church to reach out into the community is through its ministry to sick people. What a marvellous opportunity for people to care for each other. Admittedly, we did 'jump the gun' with this ministry in Yarraville.

To train our special ministers, I gave an introductory session to the people who had been invited to take Communion to our sick people. I stressed that the rubrics, or rules, must centre around whatever the people had prepared. For example, if there was a candle on the table, light it; if a bowl of water was on the table, use it. On the other hand, if nothing was prepared, don't worry.

When Ivor Wood returned from taking communion, he was worried whether he had done the right thing. On his arrival with communion, the elderly lady was watching 'Mass For You at Home' on television. She was about to turn off the television, but Ivor stopped her. He watched the Mass with her. He said the various prayers with her, gave her the sign of peace and at Communion time, gave her the Eucharist and sat down for the thanksgiving prayers on television. He had not used any of the prayers in his little book but had simply joined in her Sunday Mass.

Ivor had done a beautiful thing. How sad it would have been if concern for rubrics and prayers had deprived this elderly lady of her weekly Mass.

Life on the beach

When I arrived in St Kilda, I was introduced to the 'Beach Boys' by Cath Stewart. One of her arrangements was Christmas Dinner down in the beach gardens for the men and women who, at that time, were sleeping out under the stars. It was Christmas dinner with the trimmings. We continued this ritual for a few years and these were fun days.

There was the year when William had the decorations. He was to decorate a certain pine tree which would be our Christmas tree. We set out our dinner, had a lovely time, but kept wondering what had kept William. Eventually, we found William. He had decorated a tree alright, but in the wrong part of the gardens. When no-one arrived, he went off quite disappointed. Jack provided the Christmas entertainment with somersaults down the hill.

'Saltbush Bill' Mulcahy was always sleeping out in the gardens, although the local council made it a bit difficult with their efforts to make the beach and gardens a better quality tourist resort. This often meant that his 'resting place' would no longer be available as a bed.

It was sad the year we heard that a body had been found in the gardens. Cathy rang the mortuary to see if it was Bill. She was shocked to find out that it was not Bill, but another dear friend Bobby Krause. The worst was to come. When Cathy had given the description of Bill, the mortuary clerk told her to hold on a moment. Bill was in the mortuary too. He had died a couple of days earlier, also down at the beach area. It was hard to believe that both Bill and Bobby were dead. We had the task of going to the mortuary to identify both of our friends as they had no next-of-kin.

A double funeral was arranged for these two mates. They were buried at the Emerald Cemetery in mission graves. A funeral notice was placed in the daily paper for each of them. Early on the day it was published a young man rang me and said, 'That's my Uncle Bob'. It eventuated that Bob had walked away from his sister's home many years before because he didn't want to cause them any more worry. Worry? They had never stopped searching for him over the years. They were saddened to find him after his death, but happy that he had friends who loved him. Bobby had spent a fair period of time, on and off, at the Corpus Christi Community for homeless men. He had made a good number of toys and other articles in the occupational therapy programme. When the family arrived for the funeral, we arranged his many possessions in our front room. The family spent time alone in that room getting an insight into Bobby's life through these possessions. Again a touching moment.

With Bill, I gave a sermon about his life and held up the possessions which came from the police. A plastic bag containing a few odds and ends. I didn't need too many words on that day. These few insignificant possessions spoke vividly about one man, his simplicity, his isolation, his 'no links' situation. Yet he had a peacefulness which many people cannot find.

We had the privilege of a double funeral. It was appropriate that Bobby and Bill were together in our church for this final tribute. We had lost two friends. The following Christmas we decided that we couldn't go to the beach for our dinner. It would never be the same.

A special wedding

Tony and Mary were two young people both addicted to drugs and prostitution. They had been on the streets of St Kilda and had attempted various rehabilitation programs. Along with Cath Stewart, I had come to know them well over the years. We watched them struggle to get well and we watched them going down that track of addiction which leads to death. At one stage, Mary had been so ill that we were expecting her to die. Tony had been in so much trouble with the police that prison seemed to be the way out for him. Both seemed to have made a complete mess of their lives.

Time and again we assisted Mary or Tony or both to go to a centre to 'dry out' and make a new start. Each time their good intentions seemed to come to nothing. The last time they went away I remarked to Cath that we shouldn't pin our hopes too high, because the only way they could get better was to separate. They were not helping each other. How wrong can you be? It turned out that the main motivation for each one was their care and love of the other person.

After a couple of years of 'going straight' Tony and Mary announced that they were to marry. It was a great moment to be with them as they prepared for this day and to share this time of celebration with them and their families. Remembering about how emotional I felt at the wedding of Anne and Sharky (their story comes later in this book), I made sure that I placed Tony and Mary to the side while I gave my little talk. I knew I couldn't look at them eyeball to eyeball. Too much had happened in our lives together. I sat them at the side while I proceeded to talk to the congregation.

But I had made one mistake. Sitting directly in front of me were the best man and bridesmaid, namely Craig and Kerry, who had met Tony and Mary at the drug rehabilitation centre and had travelled a similar journey. As I talked I was face to face and eyeball to eyeball with Craig and Kerry, who had tears in their eyes. Again I had this enormous lump in my throat as I remembered back over the journey of Tony and Mary. However, lump or not, it was a moment to be treasured and one full of joy and struggle, achievement and let-down, but always one of faith and love.

A postscript to this story was the later wedding of Craig and Kerry. Again, this was a time of recognising the journey and the struggle for two young people from addiction to a new way of life.

Tragedy brings out love

About the time I was ordained I read a very simple book entitled *Everybody calls me Father*. It was written by a Father X. On reading it, I was fairly impressed by all the wonderful things that happened to this priest in a very short time, but I had the feeling that it was a bit over-dramatic. I remember feeling very much in sympathy with Father X after my experience with Trish Jennings.

In my first years at Sandringham, I had managed to begin both a YCW and a YCS group in Sandringham and also in Black Rock, the neighbouring parish. Trish was teaching at the Catholic school in Black Rock and was the key person for both the groups in Black Rock. Towards the end of 1970, we were arranging a combined youth gathering with a special Mass to wind up the year. It was to be a thanksgiving Mass on the Sunday evening in the Sacred Heart Church in Sandringham. Trish was the main organiser as well as being the lead guitar and lead singer. We were expecting a couple of hundred young people from both parishes along with many parents for this special gathering. Trish called at the presbytery at lunch time on the Friday to finalise a few details about the Mass.

That evening, just after midnight, I had a call from her mother. She was crying hysterically on the phone saying that Trish was dead. I went straight to her home. I was confronted by her mother weeping uncontrollably and clinging to me. Then I met her father who was trying to attack me. He blamed me for her death. In his grief, he reasoned that if Trish had not been at this YCW meeting, she would not have been on the road at this time of night and would not have been struck by those drunks on the way home. These young people had forced Trish's car off the road, and she had crashed into a pole. She was incinerated in the car. Trish was twenty.

It was a long night at the Jennings' home. I went with her uncle to identify her remains at the city morgue. On the way back to Sandringham, I stopped at the scene of the accident. There was nothing to see except a pole that showed scorch marks and a few skid marks on the road. I arrived home just in time to say the morning Mass for the sisters at the convent. I went to inform the sisters because Trish was one of the teachers at their school. Then I proceeded to get ready for Mass. I was doing well by this stage. However, as soon as I began the Mass that was being offered for Trish and came to the words praying for the repose of her soul, I broke down and walked from the altar. There was panic among the sisters, but all I needed was a few minutes to come to grips with the loss of Trish in my own life. Then I was able to proceed to offer Mass for her.

Those next days were very draining on me personally. So many young people were shattered by the sudden death of this young woman. The Sunday night Mass, instead of being thanksgiving for our year together, was a Mass of thanksgiving for Trish. Monday evening was the rosary and Tuesday was the Requiem Mass. Through all of this time, I was giving of myself to young people who were suffering.

Trish's father asked me to make sure it was a short service. I said that it could not be a short service because so many people loved his daughter, and that he was going to be amazed to find how far-reaching her love for others had been. I remember standing at the graveside after the funeral and her father, Perce, standing next to me saying, 'I didn't know how many people loved her'.

I made a big mistake during this time. I believed that my role was to support everyone and to be the source of strength for people. I was the priest. I was the one who had this great faith and understood. What I didn't own was that I was also suffering very deeply, and I didn't convey this to anyone. Instead, I suffered this hurting love alone. I haven't done that since. I am always prepared to let people know how much I am hurting because of the love I have felt for someone who has died.

A local character

Albert Logan was one of the characters of St Kilda. We knew very little of Albert's past except that it had taken him to the centre of Australia, Alice Springs, Coober Pedy and the rest. In some ways he was a little eccentric, in other ways he was quite learned about many subjects. He had an interesting background, but we only received little glimpses of this. He had a privacy that he was determined to hold on to. For some years Albert had been a regular at our Mission, sitting in our kitchen or yarning to people. He was always keen to sit and talk. He was a gentle person, basically a quiet person, sensitive and kind. He could also be a stubborn person! He certainly was one of the characters of St Kilda with his long hair and beard which had various colours of the rainbow in it—grey, white, ginger and nicotine stains.

Albert became ill, but he wouldn't share with us or anyone the extent of his illness. We knew from the doctor that he probably had cancer and that it was probably terminal. We always felt that Albert knew exactly what was wrong with him but was not letting us know. Sister Angela Kennedy, one of our team, took on the special care of Albert and visited him regularly in his little room at a rooming house. With Albert she went through all the stages of caring—happiness, frustration, anger, despair, hopelessness etc. On occasions, when Sister Angela could not get the message clear to Albert, because in Albert's words, she was a woman and therefore obviously did not understand, I would be called in to read the 'riot act'. Eventually there came the time when Albert needed to go to the hospital. We were able to have him admitted to Bethlehem Hospital where he would receive all the needed care and attention.

There were some memorable moments at Bethlehem. Such as the anointing of Albert when quite a few of the team attended with me. I began by hearing his confession, then we all shared the Eucharist together and I anointed him and said the prayers for sick people. It was a great spiritual celebration. When this was over, we brought out the lemonade and cream cakes to continue the celebration. When the sister walked into the room, she was somewhat taken aback. She had never been to an anointing party before! I believe that such occasions centre around people such as Albert. This gentle man died peacefully. We took care of all the funeral arrangements, and Albert was buried at Emerald Cemetery. Here he lies with many other people whom we have known around the Mission.

Where is your wife?

One of my favourite stories concerns a young girl named 'Laura'. It was a little after 1 a.m. when young Laura, who worked in prostitution on the street because of a drug addiction, came to the Mission House for a cuppa and a chat. We were chatting away quietly over a cuppa when she asked, 'Where is your wife tonight?' I explained to Laura that I was not married and did not have a wife, but she maintained that she had seen me with my wife. She was referring to Cathy Stewart who worked and lived at the Mission. I explained that Cathy was not my wife. Laura then asked, 'Is she your girlfriend?' To this I replied 'No'. I went on to explain that I wasn't married because I was a priest. Her reply was hard to beat, 'You know, Ernie, I don't think it's fair, that just because you want to be a priest and work in the church, you have to be sterile!' Oops! I replied to Laura that at times it might be a good thing if I were sterile, but I really think that she meant celibate!

On one occasion I was walking down the street towards my home one evening, when I came across young Laura. I said that I had thought of getting a special medal made for her because I felt she deserved recognition. She asked me why, and I said that I considered her to be the hardest working girl on the street and deserved a medal. She laughed a bit at this and then I asked, 'Why are you the hardest working girl on the street, Laura?' She looked at me and said, 'Well, I guess I've got the biggest habit to support'. She was referring to heroin of course. I then asked her, 'Laura, how old are you?' She replied, 'Sixteen'. At that point of time I felt as if someone had given me a good kick in the stomach. It hurt. I walked on to my home where we had a visitor, Father Hugh O'Sullivan from Adelaide, staying with us. I told him about this little episode and said, 'You know, Hughie, I just feel like crying at these times'.

The circus came to town

There was the time the circus came to town. A joyous and simple occasion was the baptism of 'Justin'. He was the child of the trapeze artists who were members of the Perry Brothers Circus which happened to be in Yarraville at this time. We received an introduction into the very different way of life of circus people. They are always on the move and don't stay long in any one place. After meeting with the parents, the Baptism was arranged for a Monday morning because that was the day off for the circus. Again we had the chance for hospitality. After all, these circus people spend their lives wandering from town to town, entertaining audiences whom they rarely meet.

We arranged to have the baptismal party at the parish centre. There they would be our guests. A very pleasant Monday morning was had by all of us from the parish team and from the circus. When I first met Bob Perry, I was given a bundle of complimentary tickets to be used by families unable to afford a seat. More than fifty people enjoyed this generosity. It was good for us to have the chance to respond with similar generosity.

Night of the fire

In St Kilda the sounds of police, ambulance and fire sirens are part of the music of the streets and the area. After living here for awhile you don't even notice them, until they stop! I was turning out the lights one night about 1 a.m. when the sirens stopped and seemed to be close. I toddled out to have a 'look' and there were all sorts of lights flashing down the road from the Mission. When I arrived, I found that one of the rooming-houses was on fire. The residents were out in the street, some escaping in a hurry. Di, whom we knew well, was wrapped in a blanket only. The police were trying to get a bit of order. The firemen were trying to ascertain whether everyone was out of the house.

I suggested to the police inspector in charge that I could take the residents to the Mission and settle them down. I headed home and woke up the others. We started rounding up blankets and mattresses. In the dining room of the hall there were mattresses and people everywhere. Di fitted into my tracksuit so that helped. The front doorbell kept going until sunrise. There were firemen, police, the arson squad and then the homicide squad. It turned out that there was someone in the back room upstairs, and it was determined that the fire was deliberately lit.

Then we learned that the dead man, Clarrie McCarthy, one of our parishioners, had been asleep and had died of asphyxiation. Clarrie was one of many men who live in the rooming-houses of St Kilda because they have separated from their families for a myriad of reasons.

Meanwhile, back at the presbytery, the people were settling in to cups of coffee and toast, feeling quite at home until about 7 a.m., when we started cooking bacon and eggs for everyone— people from the rooming-house, detectives, and ourselves. There was a great supportive spirit among the people. They were concerned for each other and very upset about the death of Clarrie. In the morning, when the police and the firemen had finished their business, we began assisting with clothing and other gear and also helping people to find new accommodation.

Shortly after, some of Clarrie's family came down from interstate. Cath Stewart and I went with them to see Clarrie's burnt-out room. They had been in touch, but they did not know how he had been living because he wanted it that way. In that burnt-out room, each one found something to take away to remind them of their father. It was a sad but beautiful moment.

Where has he gone?

'Mark' lived a very similar style of life to Mel. Chronic alcoholic, very sick at a young age, past making choices, yet very lovable in his illness. On various occasions, Mark would go into hospital for a bit of help and would recover so quickly. I can confidently say that anyone who came in contact with Mark became his friend. He was that sort of a man. A cheeky grin, a gentle voice, a courtesy and respect at all times, the caring word. All these little factors made it impossible not to love Mark. Mind you, it could be totally frustrating to be with him and to try to help him. But, above all that, you had to love him in a special way.

Mark left his room and has never returned to St Kilda. There has been no contact with any friends. Where has he gone?

*   *   *

The final two stories are a little longer. They have a particular importance for me personally. They also highlight the foundation of so much of the care carried out by the Church in both Yarraville and St Kilda.

Mary O'Hanlon's story is a reminder of the beautiful things that happen when a team of people working together are prepared to step out and take the risks involved in loving.

Bernie Stanley's story is a reminder that, wherever and whatever and however we do things, we must never lose sight of the individual person. Behind the 'big achievements' there is always the one person with whom we are called to walk in life.

Mary O'Hanlon—One special person

Towards the end of 1983 I received a long-distance phone call from a young girl named Mary O'Hanlon. She asked whether there was any way in which she could come and do some voluntary work. At that stage we were getting various requests from people who wanted to help in some way, so this was not unusual. I indicated to Mary that we could always do with a hand in the hall preparing the meals, but it seemed a long way to come from the country to peel spuds and serve meals. She replied that she was ringing from Traralgon, which is about two hours' drive from the city. She stated that she didn't mean just for a day but wished to work voluntarily in a full-time way.

I asked Mary the reason for this request. She replied she had been doing her final year at secondary school but was forced to discontinue her studies because of her health. My first thought was that she had probably suffered a mental breakdown because of the studies in her final year. I asked Mary how her health was at the present moment. She replied that she felt she was pretty good, but that the doctors at Peter MacCallum Hospital weren't so sure. Peter MacCallum is a hospital which deals exclusively with cancer. My next response was that perhaps she should come and have a talk. Mary had already told me about her involvement with YCS while a student at the Catholic college at Traralgon. She was very active in her own parish. She sounded like a lovely young person.

I let the team people working with me know that Mary was coming to see me. She sounded like a nice young lady and could probably fit in very well with our work. However, she had been receiving treatment for cancer. Perhaps this may be in remission at the present moment but could well recur. If this were to be the case, we would have to be prepared for the hurt which would necessarily come our way. We would certainly come to know and love her if she came. I received the 'go ahead' from all of the team.

Mary came and spent time with us all, stayed the night and returned to Traralgon the following day to inform her parents that she was coming to live and work with us in St Kilda. In retrospect this was a big decision. However, at the time it just seemed an ordinary response to a special request from Mary. At eighteen, Mary brought with her a bright vitality and youthful enthusiasm. Personally, I developed a particularly special fatherly role with her. We had many talks over the next few months about life and sickness.

It was around March of 1984 that Mary called me to her room to have a talk. She took my hand and placed it just above her breast and I felt the telltale lumps which indicated that her illness, namely Hodgkin's Disease, had returned. We sat together and hugged each other and cried. We then decided that Mary would go to see her doctor and confirm whether or not the disease had returned, although she herself knew the signs. When it was diagnosed, the doctor wanted Mary to return to the hospital for further treatment. But Mary made an enormous decision. She told us, both me and the doctor, that she would rather face the sickness and the prospect of dying without the treatment. She felt that this treatment destroyed her dignity as a person and did not necessarily offer a cure anyway.

I held this terrible secret in my heart for a month while, with the doctor, plans were made for Mary which could assist her in living with the illness and without treatment. It was only after a month that Mary felt she could now approach her parents and family, and speak with them. It must have been an agonising decision for Mary. Yet she carried it out with dignity and peacefulness.

The team were told that Mary's condition was to remain a secret between us all. As the months crept on, Mary did not appear any different exernally, but the telltale signs were increasing. The racking cough and shortness of breath tore all of us apart, not only Mary. Eventually Mary decided to go to an Ashram in northern New South Wales where, through diet and meditation, she would have the opportunity to experience peacefulness in herself with her God. I took Mary on that long trip to northern New South Wales, travelling by plane to Sydney where we had a few hours to walk around. By this stage Mary was lacking in energy, and we spent a couple of hours just sitting in a park. Mary rested and often fell asleep on my shoulder. We continued the journey to Lismore, where we stayed overnight with her uncle and aunt. The next day we drove to the Ashram at Nimbin. I spent the day with Mary at the Ashram. Then the time came for me to leave. That was the hardest 'goodbye' which I have ever experienced. We both knew that death was inevitable, and we both knew that this would probably be the last time we would speak to each other face to face. The farewell was a long slow one. I eventually drove off from the Ashram. It was a long drive back to Lismore, and an even longer flight back to Melbourne alone.

Two months later I received a phone call on a Saturday

afternoon to tell me that Mary had died. She had been in great spirits, experienced no discomfort and had suddenly suffered a severe heart attack while out driving with another member of the Ashram. She died instantly without any pain. The photograph of Mary taken just three days before her death, hangs on the wall of our home in St Kilda. It shows Mary full of life and vitality. It was hard to imagine that Mary had truly died. Yet we also knew that the circumstances of her death could not have been better for Mary. I rang each of the parish team to inform them of Mary's death and could just barely manage to tell each one, 'Mary has died. I'll ring you back later'. The following morning all of the team wandered into the Mission with a desire to be with each other. There was a sadness which cannot aptly be described in a few words. We were one in our love and care for Mary, and now we were one in our suffering and loss of Mary.

I well remember two of the comments made to me at the time. Eric Robertson, with children around the same age as Mary, said to me, 'You know, we have been hurt so deeply by this and yet if someone like Mary came tomorrow with the same situation and asked to work with us, we would say yes, wouldn't we?' And Avan Zarb, who had worked with us the previous year, said to me, 'Ern, you told us that if we took Mary on to work with us it would hurt. But you didn't tell us just how deeply it would hurt'.

Mary was buried at Traralgon in the country. Her Requiem Mass was celebrated on 5 October 1984, exactly one year from the day that she had come to work with us in St Kilda. It was a memorable year. The following Sunday I wrote about Mary in our parish newsletter, informing the people of her sickness. Throughout her time in the parish, people did not realise she had cancer. So her death came as a sudden shock. In the newsletter, I copied what she had written on the previous New Year's eve. At the end of 1983, moving into 1984, Mary had written her reflections on her sickness. Her reflections are worth recording here. An eighteen-year-old young woman, stricken with cancer, her active life interrupted, her studies finished, looks back over a year of the greatest trauma.

Oh Lord, it's been the most eventful year of my life. There's been pain, joy, relief, disappointment and discovery, and all of these have led to much spiritual growth. Thank you.

There has been the excitement of meeting so many new friends in January, and the uncertain anticipation of my HSC year. It took a while to settle into the pace of study. Just as I was getting used to it, I began to drag my feet. I struggled on, and only you, Lord, knew how I got through my stay in Sydney in May. I can remember wanting to leave school soon after term 2 began. I was missing days, feeling really ill, and then came the diagnosis. What was my reaction? Shock, but not really surprise.

Looking back, I was delighted at making my debut. It was a grand occasion to remember before all the slog of tests and treatment.

Peter Mac was pretty horrific, I need say no more, though the staff were very kind.

Then came the Healing Centre. I learnt so much through my stay at the Ashram and I was able to see a reason for becoming sick, otherwise I would never have discovered Yoga. I thank you, Lord, with all my soul, that you led me to Yoga for it changed my life.

I started work in the parish team at West St Kilda on October 5th and although at times I felt inadequate when faced with the immensity of the problems there, I really loved it. Help me to remember that you, Lord, were always present behind every face I served in West St Kilda and indeed everywhere.

The relief of having left school in June turned to pain,

almost jealousy, when my friends sat for the HSC exams in November. Boy, was it hard. But I couldn't contain my joy when at the HSC Cabaret I was awarded the Devlin Memorial Prize for leadership. It really helped me to relieve the hurt of not being able to complete HSC.

Christmas was pretty good. It felt like Christmas, probably because of all the preparations involved in the Sacred Heart Church St Kilda.

So now it's New Year's Eve and I'm sitting at Power's table in a toga and laurel wreath, all ready to go to a party. Things haven't quite turned out as I thought they would at my last New Year's Eve party. I must say that despite this or perhaps because of this, I have grown tremendously, especially in faith.

For the happenings of 1983, I thank you so much Lord.

Mary Sri Mataji (Dear Holy Mother)

Perhaps my own reflections at the time are worth including in the story of Mary O'Hanlon. This was given in the special supplement for our parish newsletter, along with Mary's reflection on her year.

Mary Ursula O'Hanlon 2/7/1965--29/9/1984

Mary O'Hanlon came to our parish on 5th October. Exactly one year later, requiem mass was celebrated at St Michael's Church, Traralgon.

Briefly, I would like to share this last year with the parishioners of Sacred Heart parish.

It began with a phone call from Mary, offering to do voluntary work. She was on sickness benefits following a course of treatment at the Peter McCallum Hospital for Hodgkins Disease. It was a decision for the parish team which has brought us much joy and love over the past year but also in the past months deep pain and sadness.

Mary had been diagnosed as having this illness in June, and after a short treatment at the Peter McCallum Hospital, went to a Healing Centre in Nimbin, northern NSW. Here in the life of the Ashram, under the guidance of Sri Ram, Mary learnt about yoga ... meditation and prayer, which brought her close to God and gave her a deep peacefulness.

She came to our parish team after this and entered into the life of our parish with her special vitality and joyfulness. During her work with the team, Mary came to know and love and care for many people in the parish. She brought her gift and love of music and singing, and made many beautiful contributions in this way. With particular people in the parish who needed special care and affection, Mary gave just that. Mary entered into the life of the YCW group and made special friendships in that group.

There were so many ways in which Mary became involved ... and in whatever she did, Mary took with her the greatest gift, and that is herself. It may appear that Mary was a very competent young lady but there were many times during the past year that Mary was really a frightened, young 18-year-old girl with big decisions to make. About the end of March this year, Mary discovered that the sickness had emerged again, and she shared this secret with myself and Sri Ram for a couple of weeks. During this time she agonised over the question of further treatment and finally decided against further treatment. This was a hard moment for her. As part of this decision she then went to the Ashram in late May. It was my privilege to accompany her to the Ashram and so meet Sri Ram and the other members of this beautiful community.

Here she stayed in peace and tranquillity, spending several hours each day in meditation and coming closer to the God in whom she had the utmost faith. Her health had been stable, her spirits were joyful, and overall it was a beautiful four months.

Last Saturday, while travelling from one Ashram to

another by car, Mary collapsed in mid-conversation and died.

Two weeks before she died, Mary had said to Sri Ram, 'Well, if God wants me now, I think I am ready to go'. Premonition? Probably not. Rather a statement of total peacefulness in herself and with all the people in her life.

The suddenness of her death saddened us all, but the peacefulness of the past year gives us cause to thank God. Thank you, Lord, for the way you have loved Mary and brought her peace and contentment.

Thank you to all the parishioners who have been part of Mary's life in this past year. I speak for Mary's family and for the parish team.

Father Ernie

Bernie Stanley—The long road back

One of the many lessons taught by Cardinal Cardijn through the YCW formation was very simply, the DIGNITY of each individual person. He himself had shown me how to do this by the care and concern which he showed for me and my family as we talked over breakfast in Brussels so many years ago. The message from this great leader, by his example, was that no-one is more important than the person you are with at this particular moment. This sounds easy when you say it in a sentence, but it's not so easy to practise. Can I give the person with me at this moment my undivided attention?

There always seem to be so many pressing matters, important things to be done soon or great things which have just happened. But forget the pressing matters and concentrate. Jesus tells us that he is present in this person and no-one but us can reach that person. It's hard, but it's also true.

The importance of one person is evidenced in the story about my close friend, Bernie Stanley. Bernie was one of the first people I met when I arrived at Yarraville in 1975. He was also one of the first to make himself 'at home' when Thelma and I moved to the new parish centre in 1976.

Bernie and his family were regulars at St Augustine's Church. But when his wife died in tragic circumstances, Bernie was left with three young children. Then things didn't go too well. He had fallen victim to drink, and his children were raised by other members of the family. At this time he had not seen the children for some years. For more than fifteen years Bernie had been 'down', but he never lost his faith in Mary or his love for his church. He prayed all the time to Mary, even in his worst times. Regardless of how he looked or felt, Bernie somehow managed to be in the church on most mornings, sitting towards the back by himself. He never received the sacraments. Reminiscent of the gospel parable, he sat towards the back, alone, saying his own prayers.

At this time, Bernie was sleeping outdoors quite often. He was drunk much of the time. He used to take care of the gardens around the presbytery, empty the rubbish bins in the school and do a few odd jobs around the place.

When we moved to our house up the road, into what we called the parish centre, our relationship with Bernie took on a new meaning. He took a great interest in the parish centre from the very beginning. Soon he was cutting the grass, putting a few plants in, looking after the rubbish bin and so forth. Sometimes he would simply sit out in the yard reading the newspaper or a book. He had begun to settle in.

Bernie began to have dinner with us each day. But outside in the shed! I'm sure that Thelma and I felt this separation more than Bernie. It was so uncomfortable to be sitting inside while he was outside. However, he was very comfortable, sitting outside, reading the paper while he had his lunch. He wasn't ready to come inside.

For some time, I had been trying to tempt Bernie into a bath, but there always was some excuse. Whenever we agreed on a 'bath day', Bernie would conveniently disappear. However, patience always wins and eventually we had success. The bath was filled and Bernie was innocently pottering around the garden. I innocently walked up and told him that there was some bad news. The bath was ready and waiting, and he had no excuse. After a good soak and scrub, followed by a haircut from Thelma and a new outfit of clothes, Bernie emerged a new man. This was only the beginning of what was to be a painful trek back to a new life for Bernie.

After this bath, Bernie felt that he could now share a meal at our table. We started to get together a wardrobe of clothes for him, although sleeping out didn't help things too much. From this day, the bath, shave and haircut became regular parts of life.

Christmas dinner in 1976 was arranged at the house mainly for the sake of Bernie, who had no family. It was a great celebration with all the trimmings and became a regular event at the house. Meals, baths, haircuts and celebrations were all ways of sharing life together. These were all ways of saying to Bernie, you are a worthwhile person.

Not all the times with him were forward movements. There were some rough times. We spent many hours with him sitting and yarning, reminiscing, arguing and copping the occasional bit of abuse. When Bernie was drunk, he would usually get away by himself, and this was a blessing for us. Now and again, there were some pretty nasty arguments, mostly centering around drink. There was the time when I found his hiding place for drink, and also when I found that he had been raiding my cupboard to get the sherry. These necessary but unpleasant moments fade with time because of the many good and happy times.

With all the ups and downs, Bernie was progressing along slowly until 6 May 1978. That day he found himself locked in the schoolyard on a Saturday afternoon. He attempted to climb the wall, fell off and broke his leg. What a great day!

We looked for him for three days. Eventually, on the Tuesday evening, we found him in the hospital. Next morning I asked the sisters at the convent to pray for Bernie who was in hospital with a broken leg. My prayer was that he would have a really good broken leg which would take a long time to get better! Sure enough, the prayers were answered. Bernie was in traction for a couple of months which necessarily involved 'total abstinence'. This gave him the opportunity to make a new start in life.

Thelma was so happy about another thing. On the Friday, Bernie had a bath, shave and haircut and also a new set of clothes. He was admitted to the hospital looking quite smart and certainly not in any way your usual 'down and out' person. He lapped up the attention and care. After a few weeks, he was transferred to a geriatric hospital for convalescence. During this time, Thelma and I kept up our visiting Bernie. Colleen, Joan and Veronica were also in touch with him through this rehabilitation because we had become one 'family'.

After five months in these two hospitals, Bernie went to Corpus Christi Community in Greenvale which provides 'home' for about ninety homeless men. This was to be, in Bernie's words, his 'country residence' for the next four years. Here he had a room of his own, plenty of lawns and garden to work in, some friends to care for and be cared by, Mass and Communion at the chapel, the sisters and the priests. Although he was drinking on and off through this time, he improved much over the four years.

When I went overseas in 1979 for three months, the close bond established between us meant that I sent him a postcard from every place I visited. In 1980, we went for a holiday to Sydney, driving up the highway. On this trip, there were so many highlights for a man who had never been more than fifty miles from Melbourne. I saw things for the first time because Bernie pointed them out to me as we drove. Everything was new and exciting and spoke of history to him, who is well read. This was to be the first of many holidays together.

In 1982, we went to New Zealand for a month. On our return home, we came head on with a big question. Bernie was to be 'put out' of Greenvale for awhile because it was felt that he needed to drink. But Bernie was scared and didn't want to leave, so he came to St Kilda to live with us at the presbytery. He is still living with us ten years later.

Around the St Kilda mission house and school, the gardens are always neat and tidy, and a source of peacefulness and enjoyment to many people. This is Bernie's contribution to our life. There have been many special memories over the last ten years of life together in St Kilda.

Why write so much about one person? Well, I guess that the message for me is that every person is an individual and important. It wouldn't matter how many people we see or care for if we are not caring for the people nearest to us. We cannot measure our work in hours or numbers of people. Bernie is important to me. Our holidays are important. Our living together is important. Because we are talking about people, not people by numbers, but people as individuals.